The Love Paradox

Lead Other By Loving Your Self

Karl Galik

The Love Paradox:
Lead Others By Loving Your Self
by Karl Galik

Printed in the United States of America

ISBN 9781606478110

www.xulonpress.com

Your well-being is
our blessing!

Peace, Karl

Matt 22.39

To Marilouise,
the wife of my youth
who delights with her sheer presence.

Forward

ട്യൂ

The precise moment that God chose to intersect my life with Karl Galik's was the very example of divine timing. My beloved wife Cathy had just passed away at 37, leaving me with three kids and a cynical heart. Karl found me, wrapped his pastoral arms around me and walked side-by-side with me as I navigated the forest of grief.

Eventually we became friends. Pastor Karl made church palatable for this cynical man. His messages each Sunday were something special. Never content to simply read from prepared notes, Karl spoke more from the heart than the pulpit. Using Scripture and common sense, he painted biblical portraits that were beautiful and nuanced. Of course not every one was a da Vinci, but there was always artistry and passion. And every so often, genius.

It wasn't that he had a special insight into the Bible, or that he developed a unique, never-discovered interpretation of it. It was simply that when Karl Galik talked about Holy Scripture, it made me, and others, thirst for more. It literally drew us closer to the Word. For that alone I will always be grateful.

After a time, Karl asked me to help him turn his doctoral thesis into something that regular folk could enjoy. (If you've ever had the experience of reading a doctoral thesis, either you are an egghead academic type, or you've lost a bet with someone!)

I jumped at the chance to work closely with the man who had shepherded me through the most difficult time of my life. His wisdom and constant example of living his faith made me crave our time together. It felt as though I was getting my own private seminary experience and I loved it. Karl, of course, did all of the biblical heavy lifting while I listened and nodded and offered trivial suggestions; just enough to keep me in the room a while longer. Mostly, I leaned back in my reclining leather chair and let it all sink in.

The providence of it all was not lost on me. As my life was being redirected, the Lord used Karl to slowly turn my grief-walk into a faith-walk. He used his gifts to teach me the principles in this book. Through his insights I gained a newfound ability to first manage myself well. In the midst of my darkness a new vision and mission took form and I began to move forward through faith.

Now that you have this book in your hands, I encourage you to do the same.

Michael Spehn
Author, *The Color of Rain*
Rochester, MI
July 2011

Table of Contents

Your Well-being Their Blessing Blog & Online Community

Workbook to *The Love Paradox*

Encouraging Key Relationships

Inviting You to Live Well

Multi-media Resources

Available Workshops and Speaking Engagements

Acknowledgements

Thank you to my wife, Marilouise. Your deep-waters spirit that loves God passionately has blessed me immensely.

Thank you to my children, Karla, Charlie and David for thriving in God's mission in life with Greg, Beth and Ann. Your love for God and life produce deep fulfilling satisfaction.

Thank you to Dad and Mom who illustrated the blessings of family and hard work that have shaped my soul. You have shown me it can be done!

Thank you to my friends who have loved me as "Karl" respected me as "Pastor" and pretty much ignored the fact I became "Doctor." You gifted me with room to be who I am.

Thank you to my mentors like Pete Steinke who led the way. I am standing on your shoulders.

Thank you if ever you called me Pastor and if I have ever served you in delightful or painful times. You are a part of my life in ways impossible to describe.

In an ongoing effort to continue the practice of a Biblical love of self in order to serve our neighbor, the web site, "KarlGalik. com" will continue to add inspirational resources designed to encourage the love paradox.

Thank you Lord for loving me that I can love these and more.

Introduction

The only way to live is to die.

In order to gain control, you have to let go.

In order to love your neighbor, you have to love yourself.

These are examples of a paradox.

Paradox is a truth that sounds contradictory, if not absurd. Your initial response is to say, "No, that's not right."

Instead of the statements above, you want to say the only way to live is to just do it.

Common sense says you gain control by holding on and not letting go.

And after all, doesn't the Bible say love your neighbor instead of yourself?

The beauty of many a paradox is that it only makes sense when you journey beyond the obvious apparent contradictions to the deeper but not so obvious truth. A paradox typically doesn't make sense until you've had a chance to try it out yourself. Once you get a feel for it, you'll start nodding your head and saying, "Oh, I get it."

The Love Paradox is my invitation to you to try this paradox on for size. *You will best love your neighbor as you love yourself.* Come on! See what this feels like. I know it doesn't sound right at first, but when you get a feel for it, you'll discover it is a truth that will make a life-changing difference for you. In fact I believe it will provide a freedom and confidence that really looks good on you.

Still perhaps the best part is that it will make a life-changing difference in the lives of those you love. That's right – *they* can be changed for the better when *you* have a great relationship with your self. This is also true of the people you lead. The truth is your organization or team or family will work better when you first manage yourself well.

Think about what happens to families when a dad abuses himself with alcohol. You know what happens – the whole family suffers. Think of what happens when a wife abuses herself by doing the work for everyone in the family. You know what happens – the marriage begins to splinter even before anyone notices. Think about what happens when a seventeen year old abuses himself with online distractions and endless hours in front of a screen. You know what happens – healthy relationships begin to fade, grades drop. Parents have to intervene and the entire family is impacted.

In these and countless other ways problems arise in marriages, families and organizations. All of them are rooted in poor self-management, or some form of not caring for self.

I don't want this suffering for you. I really don't. It's needless. It doesn't have to be. Instead, I want you to discover the beauty, substance and power of this paradox. When practiced, this apparent contradiction will provide the freedom and confidence you've been looking for.

In order to love your neighbor, you have to love yourself. This isn't pop psychology or the latest theory debated on talk shows. Instead it is an ancient Biblical truth - true everywhere, all the time. God has designed a marvelously interwoven network of life that blesses others when you're blessed. He has set things up so that the freedom Jesus has provided for you frees up others as well. As you gain confidence in God's design, the people you love and lead will grow more confident as well.

I know. I am a recovering over-functionary. In efforts to make good impressions, move ahead too quickly or accomplish goals instead of build relationships, I have hurt my family and hindered the mission where I have served. I know what's it like to try and get ahead at work while family priorities fall behind. I have experienced the burnout of too much work and too little renewal. In the end everyone suffered – my family and the mission I was called to advance. But, by the grace of God, I also figured it out. That "over- functionary" life doesn't work – for anyone.

The truth of *The Love Paradox* is not only ancient Biblical truth and good science – it also simply makes good sense when you take the time to think about it. This truth is a lot like gravity. It is a universal truth affecting everyone everywhere all the time. Like gravity, it doesn't depend on your belief in it to work for you! Having said that, as a Christian pastor, I do believe the freedom won for you through Jesus' crucifixion and resurrection is the only true and lasting way to love and value yourself as God has loved and valued you. Frankly, my hope is that point will be illuminated throughout *The Love Paradox*. Yet even if it does not persuade you toward a relationship with Jesus, I hope the principles will bless you to bless others.

To love others as God loves you is not a radical notion for a Christian. And frankly, it just sounds like a cliché more acceptable than a call for a Biblical love of self. This book is about why that is a problem. *The Love Paradox* is designed to lead you from the awkwardness of appropriate love of self, to accepting God's love for you - personally. It will invite you on a journey from self-doubt and fears to freedom and confidence to approach God and love and lead others more fully – more passionately. This book will illustrate how your care for your self is a part of God's grand design. It is a journey from inescapable depletion to the undeniable grace of God to live in freedom and confidence.

Try this. Before you read this book, sit down and imagine you're in a small group of friends in warm and secure surroundings. (Better yet, find such a group.) I would love for you to be with people who love you, and whom you love back. I hope you have a few people that can show trust and acceptance of one another. Now, have one of your trusted friends stand behind you with his/her hands on your shoulders. (Here, light shoulder massage may be applied.) Now you, the person seated, introduce yourself to the group – as though the person standing behind you is Jesus doing the introducing! It's that simple and that profound. It instantly and sometimes dramatically raises a number of questions. What would he say?

Presumably Jesus is someone who knows all about you, and loves you still. Would he show acceptance of your dark side? Here's someone from whom nothing is hidden, and yet he loves every part of you. Would he look past times you've been unloving? Here's someone who has paid an unimaginable price out of desire to be together with you. How would that show itself in his introduction of you?

I've seen people challenged to the point of becoming speechless. I've seen people moved to the point of tears. I've witnessed a profound impact as Truth touches the spirit. So go, try it. Tell your friends how this Friend would introduce you.

Yes, even the impact of that introduction can be transforming. This is the impact this book can have on you. The key relationship between you and Jesus, and between you and your self impacts everything else. The news media is full of people who, driven by their own self-loathing, have acted out violently. The opposite extreme is also true. The news is just as full of people who in "self-centered" loving have progressed from neglect into abuse of others for their twisted satisfaction. Yet, God's intended gift of a love of self – the way he loves us – has populated a world of people on a loving mission.

You'll begin where failure leads and renewal is born – in depletion. You'll discover the universal network of relationships and marvel at the mystery and power of real presence. You'll practice encouraging growth with balance and learn how you were composed for a rhythm that renews.

You will discover how you can:

- Remove doubts and fears and take in freedom and confidence
- Love your self more like God loves you
- Value your self more like God values you
- Live as someone loved and valued by God

When you live loved and valued by God, you will experience

- Improved relationships
- Greater impact in loving and leading others
- Enhanced inner strength through trying times
- Deeper desire for the rhythms of renewal

Everything depends on loving your self as God loves you.

I really hope you'll take the journey!

Karl Galik
KarlGalik.com

Chapter 1

About Depletion

"Only entropy comes easy."
-Anton Chekhov
(Russian Born Short Story Author)

From the Latin root, *to empty,* depletion is generally what happens "naturally" to you over time. It may also overwhelm you quickly. Overall depletion is what leaves you dry, spent and bankrupt. Depletion screams failure. Words like "burned out" or "exhausted" are used to describe the depleted experience. Usually people speak in terms of depletion of energy. There isn't enough energy where you want it when you want it.

Where there is failure, it is often the result of someone who was depleted. Maybe you yelled at the kids at the end of a long day. You were depleted. Maybe you missed the numbers on the spreadsheet that would have warned of the overdraft. You were burned out. Perhaps you forgot to place your online prescription order in time and now have to pay double for the medication. You were exhausted. Your body's fight against cancer has left you hanging on day-by-day – depleted.

It's at this point those selling "energy" target the depleted. There are energy drinks and formulas to give you energy for a few hours. There's big money in energy drinks with scary sounding names, or "energetic" names that sound like fast cars or flowing electricity. Caffeine comes dark roasted, with frothing milk, or with caramel flavoring in carbonated water. You can get it with or without sugar.

Regular Starbucks customers have an energy-seeking language all their own. You can have a Java Chip Frappuccino with a shot of syrup. If you add a shot of espresso, though, it becomes an Espresso Frappuccino. To take it one level higher, you can have it "affogato style" – meaning the espresso shot comes with mocha or caramel on top. Ask a Barrista – who has had to place an order for what some consider the longest Starbucks special order on record. I think it was a six shot, venti, 6 pump white mocha, 6 pump raspberry americano with whip cream... now if that doesn't wake you up... try a quad iced venti soy upside down extra caramel, caramel macchiato or grande iced half caf triple mocha latte macchiato.[1]

Clearly Starbucks and others are targeting depletion and trying to fill it up with some form of energy quick fix. This is profitable because it seems like everyone is running out of energy. When was the last time you heard someone say they had energy to spare – and they weren't on an infomercial?

This book is not another quick energy fix promise. This is not another snake oil elixir that's on sale if you buy now. Rather this book seeks to acknowledge universal principles that will provide the energy you need in order to love and lead others. It is designed to strengthen the powerful connection between your wellbeing and your mission. In depletion, this connection suffers and, consequently, your mission suffers.

As you discover this connection strengthened, you're really going to love it. It will set you free for leading with greater purpose and doing the hard work of love. You will be released from the self-imposed obligations of guilt. You will be empowered to do this by practicing a Biblical love of self in the way God intended.

The constant pursuit of quick fixes is the enemy to overcome. It's an enemy that takes on many forms in the lives of those stretched between guilt and pleasure, selfishness and selflessness. If you're living the day-to-day frustration of bouncing back and forth between caring for others and trying to care for yourself, this book will renew you.

In the paradox of God's incredible design, these two relationships – the one you have with God and the one you have with your self - can transform your depletion into life over-abundant. The Bible describes this transformation as mourning into dancing and death transforming into life. (Jeremiah 31.13) Depletion cannot always be avoided – but it can be *converted* into something more than you could ask, think or imagine. (Ephesians 3.20) It is crazy to seriously believe you can live a life free from depletion. All the abdominal crunches in the world can't keep you from getting old. Exercising and eating right can make aging a more rewarding experience, but it cannot diminish the grief from the death of a loved one. Depletion is a constant in our world, but so is renewal!

Here is where life with God is so amazing. Although quality of life is enhanced with good stewardship of self, in the end, it only delays or enhances the time before your ultimate depletion – death. It is here, in death itself and in all the depletions that you suffer, that God meets you and converts ultimate depletion to his glory and your good. Depletion is his canvass on which he paints the story of his love for you. It is this portrait you can take with you to remember how loved and valued you are – depleted or not.

What does this mean?

Depletion is unavoidable. Since depletion usually contributes to failure, it's critical to find a source of replenishment. Depletion just happens in life. It comes naturally from living. It comes more quickly from living without renewal. In God's plan, depletion can also be amazingly converted to a Source of strength for each new day.

What can you do?

Whenever possible - manage depletion. First you'll need to be aware enough to notice it. Then you'll have to intentionally decide whether you'll manage it or allow it to manage you. If you choose to manage it, you'll need a Source that doesn't deplete when you draw from it. That Source is the love of God found in the person of Jesus who brings freedom and confidence to love and lead. He is your overflowing Source for renewal. Strangely enough when you are most depleted you are usually the most ready for God's renewal. It's called a paradox.

Chapter 2

The Story of Ultimate Depletion

"My God My God, why have you forsaken me?
- A Psalm of David (22.1)

What does depletion and Jesus' crucifixion have to do with one another?

Why has the crucifixion become so central in history? Why is it so unique in world religions?

What happened to Jesus that is different from the sacrifice of countless soldiers and martyrs in history?

What did Jesus mean when he asked the Father why he had been so forsaken?

How does Jesus' crucifixion in Israel thousands of years ago provide a non-depleting source for you?

God loved, so God gave.

As a therapist and pastoral counselor, I have learned the critical importance of asking the right question. The right question stirs the imagination and leads to new thinking. It can turn down the heat of reactivity and encourage thoughtful responses.

However, asking the right question is far more than a therapeutic tool. A good question not only calls you to participate in a deeper discovery process, but can illustrate the care, love, and concern of the one asking the question. If I ask one of my adult children, "What is it you truly believe?" The question not only calls on them to consider a deep-seated truth, but informs them of my interest in their spiritual life. The discussion from these questions typically leads to great family discussion.

In the Gospel of Matthew alone, Jesus asks about eighty questions. Many challenge you to consider why there is such a lack freedom and confidence. *"Who of you by worrying can add a single hour to his life?"* (Matthew 6.27) The last question he asks in this Gospel frames the incredible love he has for you by suffering unimaginably for your sake. *"My God, my God, why have you forsaken me?"* (Matthew 27.46)

Simply overhearing Jesus' anguished inquiry to his Dad provides insight into the nature of the gospel and the nature of his sacrifice. It gives insight into the crucifixion seldom considered. There was far more than physical torture endured by Jesus. There was a depravity suffered as a result of horrible abandonment. The question of Jesus from the cross reveals what the casual observer could not see. There was so much more than physical suffering and so much more than "typical" love for you that could not be easily understood during this gruesome moment.

The overheard question from the cross calls you to even deeper spiritual discovery of the nature of this intimate Father-Son relationship. It reveals Jesus' trust of the Father in allowing the horror of a crucifixion, believing all the while he will raise him up again. This question from the cross also demonstrates the extent of what the Father would do for you – abandon his Son to what would have been your fate. Together, the Father and the Son's powerful care, love and concern for you is spoken in the Father's tender relationship while still committing his Son to a violent, even vile death.

Without question, the physical torture that led to Jesus' death was horrid. As a clear illustration of man's inhumanity to man, the torture of the Roman soldiers and the crucifixion itself depicts physically what the spiritually depleted heart expresses invisibly. The soldiers, and those who placed Jesus into their hands, expressed their hatred in everything from spitting to throwing punches at him. The tortuous expressions of malicious spite were seen in the whipping and mocking by overzealous soldiers. The piercing pain of nails through flesh and the slow depletion of breath through suffocation that was a part of crucifixion are unimaginable and unfathomable. The fact that they are fueled by a venomous hatred is even more difficult to describe, much less understand.

Still, a much worse spiritual horror occurred behind the scenes. It was the abandonment of the Son by his Father. What crucifixion is to physical suffering, abandonment is to the soul. Stories of abandoned babies found in terrible places produce a shiver of disbelief about the cruelty displayed in such a horrible way. If you've suffered the betrayal of a spouse, you understand abandonment's pain on the soul. If ever a friend suddenly turned on you, or a coworker walked away to let you take the blame, you have felt the pain and confusion of abandonment. If you've ever been shunned because of the false rumors of others, you have a sense of the loneliness of abandonment. A good friend of mine once called me at the airport to let me know I shouldn't come back to work for reasons he wouldn't explain despite great progress on the current project and exemplary accomplishments. I have felt the sting of betrayal and abandonment. It hurts.

The abandonment Jesus suffered was part of the plan to get you back; to pay for all of life's abandonments. Far beyond physical suffering, Jesus was abandoned to suffering induced by hatred. Realized in the eyes of callous soldiers, Jesus would subject himself to humanity's cumulative abandonment – even by his Dad – for your sake. There was physical pain, yes. But how much more is that magnified in abandonment? There was abandonment by friends who would run, but how much more painful when the last to turn away is your Dad?

Where is this place where horrid physical pain is prevalent? Where is this place where abandonment is the norm? Where is the only place the presence of God is absent? This is the place found in Jesus' crucifixion. The plan would be for Jesus to suffer the impaling pain of God's absence. No matter how you describe it or what you call it, it is as horrific as suffering gets.

Jesus screamed, *"My God, my God, why have you forsaken me?"* because that was the plan and this was the execution of the plan. The quote of Psalm 22.1 ties it into ancient history. Physical pain, while suffering abandonment, is but the gateway to be spiritually, ultimately forsaken. All this and more took place then, there, for your benefit now.

The purpose? *You are his purpose.* Jesus volunteered for unspeakable pain to be certain you might have the opportunity to never know the hell of ultimate depletion.

Although I raised my children imperfectly, I gave them many gifts. Many of these gifts they will never fully realize. I did not abuse alcohol or drugs, so my children never experienced the painful and twisted environment of addiction in a family. They have listened to friends describe such traumatic childhood homes, and although they can empathize and love, they cannot feel in their soul the pain and confusion of addiction in a family. Along with my wife, Marilouise, that is our gift to them. Whether my grown children ever stop and realize that is secondary to the joy of giving them the gift.

Such is the nature of the gift Jesus has given you. You do not have to ever know the deepest abandonment there is because he suffered it for you. You do not have to ever experience the terrible absence of God because he chose to take your place for that which was headed your way. Such ultimate and unspeakable suffering doesn't have to happen to you or anyone from then on, from now on.

The crucifixion of Jesus is the suffering of depletion to ultimate degrees. The resurrection of Jesus is the opposite. It provides the freedom and confidence that your price has been paid and you are now free to be free. Ultimate depletion itself was ultimately depleted. It is the death of ultimate death. Having trusted his Dad to bring him back from the depths, Jesus returns with unfailing and unending resources. For this reason you can live in rhythms of renewal. When you run out, or become run down, Jesus, as resurrected Lord, remains the Source to defeat depletion. He's become the go-to person when conflict and discord deplete a relationship. The forgiveness he's won and brought back restores what might otherwise bankrupt a relationship. When futility and meaninglessness sneak into your life camouflaged like a virus, he has purpose and relationship to stimulate your spiritual and physical immune system to ultimate health and wellbeing. If/ when friends shock and betray you; you can be assured of a presence in the midst of it all. When stuff happens to you, through no fault of your own, he brings a presence of hope that refills dreams and enhances recovery.

The crucifixion and the resurrection are the epitome of real and powerful love. This is love that accepts death (and more) for our self*ish* greed. This is love that supplies the power for the formation of new relationships. This is the love that provides a new self to love and cherish. This is the love that allows you to love him back wholeheartedly, and love yourself that you might love your neighbor. This is the reason you're invited to love yourself as God loves you. Jesus' depletion makes you the steward of the gift a Biblical love of self illustrated in Jesus' question, *"My God, my God, why have you forsaken me?"*

You are so valuable and important to God that he would design a plan to rescue you from a place you could not rescue yourself. You are that loved by Jesus he would suffer horrifically so that you would never know such suffering. This is why you can value yourself the way God values you. *This is why you can love yourself as God loves you*!

What does this mean?

Jesus' crucifixion was total depletion and abandonment by his Dad so that you might forever be renewed by love. His gift was to substitute himself to suffer what would cost us eternally. The resurrection is his return with himself as the Source that never depletes. From forsaken to resurrection is now the plan to deal with depletion. By avoiding it when we can and being rescued from it when we cannot, depletion becomes converted to work for us, not against us.

What can you do?

Love him back enthusiastically. Love the Lord your God with all your heart, soul, mind and strength. (Mark 12.30) The best way to do that is to love your neighbor as yourself. Loving others minimizes their depletion and encourages trust in God's conversion of their depletion. Loving God also means loving yourself the way God loves you. It means valuing yourself the way God values you. In this way you are blessed, others are benefited and God is glorified. This is God's love paradox.

Chapter 3

Getting Passive to be Active

૭૩ઙ

"It is for freedom that Christ has set us free."
— *St. Paul (Galatians 5.1)*

Relax.
The renewal you seek is designed to be elegantly simple to achieve. God's rhythm of renewal begins in him, blesses you and then affects others around you. It begins by you being passive.

First, accept love. Accept what Jesus did for you. It illustrates how incredibly valuable you really are. Since you are so incredibly valued, accept yourself as one greatly loved and valued by God. This is the reason you can love yourself honestly and without being ashamed or arrogant. I have discovered this is harder than it sounds. As this Biblical love of self develops though, you will begin to enjoy the freedom and confidence that comes with this gift of being valued. It allows you to accept yourself for who you are, while encouraging growth in spirit and in truth.

The universal principles of *The Love Paradox* are intended to relieve you of the pressure to have to succeed. Instead of a numbered step-by-step process, it is a simple but wonderfully profound truth discovered within your self. Once discovered, it feels similar to receiving a special gift from a friend. When you receive a friend's gift your reception of it has an impact on the relationship. You unwrap it and the joy you express and the appreciation you show alters you. It may even connect the two of you through embraces. Did you ever wonder why people hug after receiving a gift? I see it as a way to illustrate externally what has happened internally. The embrace confirms to you and the gift-giver that your relationship is closer or more connected. In the same way, when you receive God's gift of love and acceptance it connects you to God, the Gift Giver. The very next thing that happens is that it connects you to those around you. It's not a formula you have to memorize. It's not something you have to do at all. You don't *have to* open a gift from a friend. You *get to* open the gift and enjoy the relationship connection the gift illustrates.

Loving yourself in order to love your neighbor engages the hidden but powerful universal rhythm that resonates throughout creation. Consider the analogy of what happens when you start using your computer. You don't see the code instructing the computer, you see the program that has been written so you can do word processing. First managing yourself well is more like the code behind it all – invisible but working at the speed of electrons on a motherboard. When you value yourself like God values you, it sheds light on this universal rhythm, this "code" at work in God's design. The universal code is the interwoven fabric of relationship and family life present and influencing you in profound but invisible ways. Loving yourself in order to love your neighbor is the "operating system" behind relationships, interactions, individuals and groups. It is the power of relationships – especially the relationship initiated by God himself.

God designed the gift of a Biblical love of self for you to have influence in both intimate and grand scales. If you have ever experienced a newly engaged woman enthusiastically raising her new ring to your face, celebrating the loving promise of commitment, you understand the impact God's gift given to you can have on everyone around you. The joy of being wooed by God can cause you to turn to others in new ways so you can feel and express the delight in the new relationship. Instead of a new ring, it's a new you!

Like any gift of God, it's optional. He does not force, but invites. Like a loved one inviting you to a dinner, he lovingly insists, but does not arm twist. Like a close friend asserting friendly influence on you to accept the blind date he set up, so God's gospel invitations are often in the imperative – he insists, but doesn't force. It is the same imperative voice of your close friend that just knows you'll like the blind date – even as you protest from your reluctance. Your decision whether to go home and watch another movie or go with the blind date set up by your friend will all depend on whether you trust your friend – or not. Does she/he *really* have your best interest in mind? Does she/he *really* know you well enough to set you up on a blind date? Do you really want to gear up for the adventure of it all or just chill after a busy week?

Funny enough, God's call for your inner transformation has some interesting parallels. It's likely you just want to chill. There is often a human reluctance to go through real transformation. You're not ready for transformation in large part because of the energy you know it would take. And, you too have to decide whether God has your best interest in his mind. You have to wonder if he knows you well enough to love you so incredibly.

Not to worry. Even if I insist on you receiving the gift, it's always a gospel invitation. As you engage the love of God and a Biblical love for yourself, and then actually manage yourself well, so those around you will be blessed. That's the beauty of the gift. You first passively accept the gift and then actively engage it in your relationships with others.

It has been my joy over decades of ministry to see people accept God's gift and renew from the inside out. It has been my multiple sorrows to see people with curmudgeon like resistance refuse to open God's gift given in Jesus. Come on, trust me. You don't *have* to open the gift, but why refuse such a thing? It's not self-help, it's God's work which helps change everything.

What does this mean?

Receiving God's gift of love calls on you to graciously accept what you did not earn, to cherish what you did not deserve to receive. For a healthy spiritual life, you become passive in order to become active. You receive in order to give. This is a central part of the gift found in life with God through Jesus. His gift of love will transform you, which, in turn, transforms others.

What can you do?

Let go *then* get busy. Rest assured *then* go for it. Step away *then* step into the middle of it. By receiving God's gift of love, you accept the costly gift given to you – freedom and confidence. Take care of the gift, the new you, and Biblically love and care for yourself – in order to love and connect with others.

Chapter 4

My Story of Recovering

ॐ

Experience is simply the name we give our mistakes
— Oscar Wilde

I grew up in a working class family near Midway airport in Chicago. I am the first born and only son with three younger sisters. My Dad is the fourth son of a Slovak immigrant. He dropped out of high school to drive a truck. My Grandpa in Chicago came to the US at age 11 and scratched out a living working in the Chicago Stockyards. He was (likely) alcoholic and physically abusive.

My Grandpa from my mom's side came over from Czechoslovakia and eked out a nominal living on a hilly dairy farm in Wisconsin. He spoke English poorly, and was a man of many sorrows. Two of his sons died in a flash flood. His young wife died of uterine cancer, and his youngest daughter was killed in an automobile accident. Even a brief intergenerational review reveals hard working immigrants and children of immigrants with minimal formal education and a strong European work ethic.

From this family and context my Dad became a bricklayer. Bricklayers and their laborers did not sit around on break and discuss how best to manage themselves well for the sake of the job they were working. No, theirs was a language and a sub-culture all its own born from the risks and hard pursuits for a better life. Self-management, however they might define that, was a conversation for someone else that had time to think about such nonsense to avoid real work.

My early lessons in life were formatted from these families and, in particular, my short summer "career" as a laborer for a bricklaying crew for which my Dad was foreman. It was a classic crew, worthy of some modern day reality TV on some desperate cable channel. One bricklayer smoked filter-less Camel cigarettes. He had been known to grunt, "You can't smoke a *f — filter."* He preferred beer to water to quench his thirst. He was thirsty from the first morning break through the rest of the summer day. Another was a physically large guy, gregarious and strong. One was older (by my twenty something standards), talked about sleeping around (he used the bricklayer's vernacular) and openly degraded women in general.

He always addressed my Dad, Charlie, as *Chal-ee* as though it were two names and difficult to pronounce. He regularly urged my Dad, to "put me on the wall" (bricklayer lingo for train me to be a bricklayer), but my Dad's answer, always the same, was like a litany practiced between them. After the older Charlie would call out to my Dad, my Dad would respond, "If he picks up a trowel, I'll break his *f —* arm." I had already declared my intention to go to seminary to become a pastor, so, as you might imagine, this basically intensified what might be called, the Chicago Bricklayers training ground. (I did find that by the time I entered the ministry, little, very little, offended me.)

Dad didn't want me to become a bricklayer. He didn't want me to like bricklaying. I would learn much later in life, he himself didn't like bricklaying, but did it for forty plus years to support his family. He did this to the tune of paying off a 20-year mortgage in 14 years. I later learned he was trying to keep me from suffering the same lifetime occupational sentence. What I saw as a young man was a physical perseverance to work through difficult climates and job circumstances. What I learned as a middle-aged man was the mental and emotional toughness needed to work through myriads of difficult circumstances for the sake of the family.

So, my family-of-origin was neither the time, nor the place for discussions about managing my energy output. There weren't discussions about balance, wellness or not working so hard. You can imagine the banter and grief that might accompany bringing this book to that bricklayer crew of those many years ago.

Yet, the universal principles addressed in this book are not about teaching those guys then or any of us now, how to find balance in work and life. That would be the software, the content or information that may or may not fit your particular context. No, without ever explaining the science of systemic thinking, this book examines the way in which such perseverance was maintained, how their operating system was working in the background to sustain them to productivity.

It was obvious Dad's crew had great working relationships. Each guy was keenly aware they had to "pull their own weight" and in their own (sometimes peculiar ways) did whatever was necessary to keep their end of the deal. When they went home, they left the job at the job site. They seldom worked Saturdays and never worked Sundays. They found renewal in Cubs games, family parties and family meals. Their mission was clear and measured in bricks laid or houses completed. Their passion was tied to their income. Work harder so you could earn more. Work harder yet to pay the mortgage off sooner.

It was from this working, blue-collar context that I was launched into the clergy collar world after eight years of college education, (although I would complete ten years of graduate studies with a total of three graduate degrees). I was clearly programmed for perseverance and hard work, but I was no longer tied into the rhythms of the working class, blue-collar world.

A thick skin meant I was equipped for pushback, but not so much for diplomacy. Hard work was a friendly companion, but in the world of congregational leadership, it was nearly impossible to measure – even harder to leave behind "on the job site." Weekends were busier than weekdays, but weekdays didn't afford opportunity for parties, and friends to gather. In a small dual-parish congregation, I was the crew pulling all the weight with no one else to pick up slack from a slipping funeral sermon or procrastinated Bible study. Basically, my salary was not tied to production (per se). So, no matter how hard I worked, my pay stayed the same.

In short, I entered congregational ministry ill equipped to manage myself well. As a result my family and I suffered even while the congregation rewarded me with kudos for being such a hard worker. The seeds of discontent were sown, partially because the family and the congregation; work and the kids; hours away and time with Marilouise, were always in conflict with one another.

One of my daughter's earliest difficult memories is a rare debate turned argument with raised voices at the dinner table. It was Marilouise trying to reason with me, to see the self-defeating course I was taking. It was toddler Karla who has the echo of her Dad yelling at the dinner table something about Marilouise not understanding why I had to spend so much time away from the family.

Likely as not, my own personal turning point came when I entered the house late for dinner and very surprised at all the colorful helium-filled balloons dancing in midair. The "Happy Birthday" streamer that hung over the kitchen table provided the small electrical charge in my brain that prompted memory to recall. It was my son Charlie's birthday party this evening. I was late. As if that wasn't bad enough, it was also my wife Marilouise's birthday. Busted!

Although the seed of my ministry was born more from my failures to manage myself well, the continued development of these principles are testimony to the way in which we all disconnect with others to pursue our own selfishness. My experience as a pastor and therapist has also led me to experience the reflex to perpetuate an independent-from-others lifestyle rather than a *Biblical love of self* that connects.

An appropriate care for self, *Biblical love of self*, serves to provide a spirit that can relate, serve and participate with others. The opposite *selfish* love acts independently of others for its own good alone, using up the resources of family, organizations, and relationships instead of connecting and contributing.

The US Department of Health and Human Services, reports that 24.3 million people experienced serious psychological distress in the past year. According to *"Stress Directions,"* a group specializing in the research and treatment of stress, it is known that stress is having a significant domino effect on first, individuals, then the organizations to which they belong and finally impacting the culture at large.[2]

The Center for Disease Control reports that stress is linked to physical and mental health as well as a decreased willingness to take on new and creative endeavors. Note its effect both outwardly and inwardly. Improper management of self impacts everything from the boardroom to the brain, from tension at the dinner table to rumors around the water cooler. *The Love Paradox* addresses a common underlying current from pastors to presidents. The greater the appropriate management of self, even during unavoidable stressful times, the less impact on the self. The less impact on self, the less impact on family, organization and even culture-at-large.

It's not as though families will have only happy faces at dinner. It's not as though boards won't struggle with difficult circumstances. Mean spirited people still seek to dominate families and organizations. Even if you first manage yourself well, these all continue to occur — but they have less impact on you and the organization when you intentionally care for yourself through the process. More important than simply taking care of yourself, and short of selfish behaviors, managing your self well is critical because of the powerful internal and external effect your interactions have on families and organizations alike. Whether it is a parent encouraging a junior high student to attend a dance or a director handling a hostile board member, mature *management of self* increases the likelihood of success in missions small and large.

The end result of loving yourself as God has loved you, permeates all levels of relationship and interactions. A Biblical love of self enhances, rather than diminishes relationships. It's the key ingredient necessary to lead as president of the PTA, President of the Board, or foreman on my Dad's bricklaying crew.

What does this mean?

To one degree or another life is a state of "recovering." Our family-of-origin sends us into life incomplete. Life is the process of recovering well. Central to this maturing process is your relationship with your self. It is important to learn to love and forgive yourself as God has loved and forgiven you to continue recovering.

What can you do?

Practice forgiving yourself and others. Gain insight from the imperfections of your family of origin, but do not use them as an excuse not to grow up. Begin with God's love for you and allow that to sustain an appropriate love for yourself. This is important to all other relationships that offer opportunity for growth or maturity.

Chapter 5

Two Kinds of Love

*"Having chosen the ravaged path of independence,
you don't even comprehend that you are
dragging the entire Creation along with you."*
—*Sarayu to Mac from The Shack*

You may notice from my story of recovery where spiritual and emotional problems originate. The general rule of thumb is, if it curves inward, it's a problem. In general such problems originate in your family-of-origin.

Although all family-of-origins are unique, a common denominator of any family is found in dysfunction rooted in selfishness. Pastors refer to this as the inward curvature of sin. Test it out and see. Sin always curves inward to serve the self. Its energy and power is rooted in selfishness

"Sin" is more than the oversimplified definition of simply doing something wrong according to a code. It is more of an orientation to perceive and behave from our personal perspective – instead of seeing things from God's perspective. You see, in the Christian lifestyle you're called on to die to self and live for Jesus. (Colossians 2.12) His calling, mission and invitation define your lifestyle post conversion.

It's the nature of the gift of baptism, to put on Christ. The word "conversion" itself describes a change of orientation, change of direction. (Acts 15.3) In God's Kingdom, you die and are re-born daily. This happens in daily decisions to trust God's larger perspective instead of reacting instinctively toward your own desires. The crucifixion and resurrection of Jesus provides the pattern for living. You trust God in order to die to self again and again. You grow to trust that God will make you more than you could ever be without his intervention. The good news is that all this happens to you, for you, and within you because of the gift of Jesus. (Romans 14.7,8)

The Love Paradox encourages this new you to continue the process of dying to self. Essentially this is the maturing process of learning to see and live from God's point of view. The mysterious work of the Holy Spirit gives direction to this new life and provides a lens to see God's universal perspective.

All theology can be summarized in this phrase, "God is God, and you are not him." I've often added the editorial, "… and I don't like it that way." I know that in your mind you know you're not God, but still somewhere in your soul, you're disappointed. This is what happens with implosive love. Like an attack of appendicitis, the pain of selfish love builds till it bursts. Left unchecked selfishness always ends in death. Selfish love is living with a self-centered orientation to life with the implied creed, "God may be God, but so am I."

Social scientists in the fields of philosophy, psychology and religion speak of this as "phenomenology" to describe life's subjective, rather than objective perspective. This thirteen-letter word has the same sense of the view of sin as "life turned inward." It's seeing life from your perspective alone. In its most basic sense, this thirteen-letter word, "phenomenology" refers to personal, sensory experiences. It is the scientific study of how your senses perceive and relay information.

For example, two people looking at the same red blotch will experience the red blotch differently for many reasons. Each person viewing the red blotch has different retina qualities that receive and interpret the color differently. Each has a specific angle and lighting that may add or diminish hue to the red. Each has a different history and experience with a red blotch. This personal history with a red blotch predisposes one person to see the color shaded by the perspective of their history. So if you, as a child had people jumping out of dark corners sticking red blotches in your face to frighten you, you might be classically conditioned to scream and close your eyes when presented with one. It would hinder, or at least alter your red blotch experience.

The point is you cannot escape your own perspective. It's built into who you are. Red blotches are silly enough to be benign, but when questions of good-bad, right-wrong, life-death and personal freedoms verses community responsibilities are tossed into the mix, it all can quickly become a confusing jumble of opinions. In each case you see things primarily from your own perspective.

I was recently listening to a podcast of an NPR segment in which an interviewer was asking people on the street whether or not there would always be wars. The overwhelming response was, "Yes, there will always be wars." The basic reason why people believe this resonates with this description of implosive love. Whether a gang member, dictator or senator, all people have sin's internal curvature at their core. Like light from a black hole cannot escape its horizon, you cannot escape the overwhelming gravity of your own perspective.

Interestingly enough, an appropriate, Biblical love of self serves to satisfy your own personal desires and look to the needs of others. An appropriate care for self, a *Biblical love of self*, serves to produce a spirit that can relate to others, serve those in need with compassion and participate with others in teams. The opposite, *selfish* love, acts independently of others for its own good. Selfish love uses up the resources of family, organizations, and relationships in general, instead of connecting and contributing. Its perspective is from itself and for itself.

In effect, there is love that turns inward (like sin) and love that turns outward (like service). Unfortunately, the identical word, *love,* can be so dramatically polar in its meaning. There is self*ish,* think-of-yourself-first love. This is the stuff that gets you stuck in the mirror, or in the reflection of those who "just adore" you. It's the love St. Paul warns his spiritual son Timothy about. (2 Timothy 3.2*f*) Paul essentially creates a compound word, *phil-autos,* expressed in English as "lover of self." This is the only time this word is found in the Bible. It's noteworthy for two reasons. First, Paul's unique use of this word highlights the trouble he's trying to warn Pastor Timothy about. He's essentially providing a catalogue listing of stuff that happens when people become *phil-autos,* a lover of self.

Although the list itself is bad enough, verse six is particularly disturbing. *"For among them are those who creep into households and capture weak women, burdened by sins and led astray by various passions."* News stories such as the thirty-two year sentencing of Dustin Patterson from Tulsa, Oklahoma fit Paul's description and bring instant angry response. Patterson was found guilty of kidnapping, burglary and child abuse on September 11, 2009. He pulled a young girl through her bedroom window early one Saturday morning. She was later pushed from the car with "only" cuts and bruises, and no evidence of molestation and quickly reunited with her family.[2]

In the extremes of *phil-autos* lover of self, a focus on one's own desires can be this pathological, this troublesome. I'm sure there is a psychological diagnosis that labeled Patterson, but to see him as *phil-autos,* a pathological lover of self, sheds new spiritual light on what happens when this *phil-autos* is unregulated. People run amok. Left unchecked, unregulated, without boundaries, a fondness of self destroys relationships and the people around them.

Secondly Paul is writing to Pastor Timothy from a prison cell. This is, in effect, St. Paul's last will and testament. He's lonely and aware he's on his final days. In this imprisoned circumstance he writes of what he believes is most important. He speaks of things for which he has strong passion. His warnings to his spiritual son, Timothy, provide insights into the dangers inherent in being in love with your self.

Further up the continuum from Patterson-like extreme behavior, we all have to be cautious of becoming a lover of self. It comes on from the hero worship of those who watched you hit the home run, land the big client or solve a Soduko puzzle quickly. When you look at yourself in the reflection of their eyes, you feel like you're bigger than you really are. Although it only lasts for a relative moment, it feels good enough to look forward to when it's there.

In stark contrast, there's love of self from-being-declared-holy, friend of Jesus, love. The Bible's phrase is, *justified by grace through faith.* It is the crux of Christianity. It is the clear distinctiveness of the gospel. It is initiated in the core of God's being. (1 John 4.8,16) The beauty of this love is its permanence, consistency through and beyond time. Jesus' crucifixion is the focal point of this love. It directed the sacrifice of God's Son to pay all penalties for every selfish form of love that kills. It means quite simply when you accept this sacrifice as your gift, you too are *declared righteous.*

Jesus' word for this Biblical *love* in Matthew 22.39, is *agapao.* This is the love of God, our Father, that causes him to sacrifice his Son that you might never know what you missed. This is the love of God delivered to the door of your soul through faith. This is the gift. In essence, you *agapao* your self that you might *agapao* your neighbor. Since this love finds no equivalent in the English language, and no landing place in the human soul, God sets up a flow of *agapao* through his Word and your faith. His Holy Spirit invigorates your spirit so that *phil-autos* is emptied and regularly replenished by *agapeo.*

The selfish love that drains you of love and light is like the vortex of a black hole. This is the "love" that blinds you to boundaries and lulls you into the arousal of lusts that build in intensity when unsatisfied. This is the light trapping quality of addiction. These addictions intensify and need to be fed more and more till less and less light escapes the home, the family, the marriage, the soul. You'll recognize it in others when you have to keep your distance to find the light of clarity. People who are in a relationship with practicing addicts are usually confused. These practicing addicts claim to love "in their own way" as an excuse for their love of darkness. This is the activity noted by the prophet Isaiah (5.20), *"Woe to those who call evil, good, and good evil; who put darkness for light and light for darkness, who put bitter for sweet and sweet for bitter."*

The opposite is love that provides abundant radiant energy. This light chases darkness away as quickly as loneliness dissipates at a lover's embrace. (John 1.1f) This light expels the darkness because the darkness cannot grasp the powerful nature of this force. This light transforms shame into a lover's delightful gaze. (Ps 34.5) This light creates thrills that last and hearts that race from basking in its energy. It's in this light and from this love that everyday pleasures take on rich and lasting satisfaction.

Selfish love implodes and collapses in on itself. It's like those massive old warehouses with precisely placed dynamite charges that explode in such a pattern as to fall straight down and land in a heap of rubble. This is the selfishness of eating without discipline or drinking without moderation. This is the selfishness of the undisciplined life, under achievement and avoidance of intimacy. Each selfish act lays one more explosive near a load-bearing wall. It could be a hand raised in drunken anger, or crossing the double yellow line while falling asleep at the wheel, or a million other possibilities, but it's likely there will come a time when the whole thing collapses in on itself in a dusty heap. People may watch and shake their heads from a safe distance, but they are helpless to reverse the implosive destruction of this dark love.

Love that builds from a firm foundation, makes interconnections that fortify the whole structure, making it strong and tall. It networks, connects, interweaves and is held together by a love the same way mortar forms the joints of bricks and binds them together for security. This is the love of interconnected strength with Jesus as the cornerstone. (Matthew 21.42; Acts 4.11; 1 Peter 2.6,7) This is the mom who prays for and spends time with her husband in order to bless her children. This is the parent who makes less money in order to make more time at home. This is the day-to-day love that builds up others one brick at a time.

There is a love whose primary purpose is to feel good. This adolescent love is measured in personal pleasure. It's defined by how good you feel at the moment. Then there's a mature love that feels good when it is living purposefully. In the deeper passions of intentional living, it feels good to be part of the higher calling, lasting effort and global mission. Yes, there's still a desire to feel good about what you're doing in any given moment, but in a more significant and lasting fashion.

There is a love that originates in discontent and always wants more.

Then there's a love that originates from perfect wholeness and never needs anything - especially more.

There is a love that is reciprocal, living *quid pro quo*. This love will scratch your back after its own back no longer itches.

Then there's a love that gracefully accommodates to scratch that unreachable itch, even when dog tired.

There is a love that is convenient.

Then there's a love that is sacrificial, ready to leave comfort zones behind in order to bring others comfort.

There is a love that clings and scratches for life, and loses more of it with each reach.

Then there is a love that gives itself away freely, all the while growing like crazy.

There is a love of self that is born from within a depleting spirit and a dying body.

Then there's a love never born, flowing from an eternal Source and providing Life overflowing forever.

There is a sel*fish* love creating gods out of the temporary and the passing.

Then there is God who is Love, tangible in Jesus, but mysterious in the Spirit.

There is a love that reflexively, instantly thinks about itself first.

There is a love that manages self, first, in order to provide for another.

If you practice the first love, you'll be looking for every excuse to put yourself first in line and use the justification that it's supposed to be good for you. If this by itself doesn't kill you, others will surely be tempted.

If you'll receive the gift of Love from the God who is Love, this stuff will intrigue, perhaps enchant you and those around you. If you'll receive Jesus and his sacrifice in your place, you'll be a steward of a sacrificial love that (curiously enough) is pleased, even rewarded by each sacrifice. If you'll receive the Spirit, your kiss of peace will be sweeter. You'll breathe easier even when life is inexplicably harder.

The Love Paradox is all about this second love – the one that is God's gift,

manages self to provide for others,
remains tangible yet mysterious,
flows from an eternal Source,
grows like crazy,
costs you dearly but pays you back even more,
is meaning-full,
horribly inconvenient,
doesn't need more,
lives purposefully,
is satisfied, radiant, and, a friend of Jesus.

It provides everything from the desire to love and the Spirit to do it. He calls and equips you to love and care for yourself, in order to love and care for others because you have been loved and cared for first. (1 John 4.19) This is the stuff that gives you life because it killed Jesus. This is the central paradox to *The Love Paradox*. First you receive the gift – God's love in Jesus. Then you manage the gift received so that you receive the blessing God intends in the giving. That, in turn, arouses others with whom you are connected.

Loving yourself in order to love your neighbor is the good love.

What does this mean?

A Biblical love of self connects you to your self and others. A selfish love disconnects. It will sever relationship connections. Selfishness always turns inward. It implodes. A Biblical love of self focuses outward. It expands. God's love connects. Selfish love severs. It's how you can tell the difference between *agapao* and *phil-autos* love.

What can you do?

Be open to receive God's love and then intentionally express it. Recognize that your point of view is severely limited by your experiences. God's Spirit empowers you to accept his universal perspective. Develop daily rituals that bring to mind God's great love for you in order to best connect with others. Check the KarlGalik.com web site for daily reminders, weekly blogs and regular webinars. Develop trusting relationships that speak the truth to you in love. In this way, you'll grow to see life from a wider perspective instead of the narrow lens of your own point of view.

Relationships Aren't Something, They're Everything

God is a God of relationships. From the most ancient information, God presents himself in relationship. He is not only in relationships with himself as Father, Son and Holy Spirit but also pursues relationship with us. First he spoke into being a creation that is woven together. Everything is in relationship to everything else. Then he creates humanity in his image reflected in male-female relationships. The procreation of life itself is tied into the most intimate of relationships.

Then when relationship is broken between humanity and God he enacts a plan to restore relationship. This is the plan and work of Jesus whose sole purpose is to reconcile the broken relationship. Then, the Spirit is supplied to sustain the relationship re-established. The sustaining of these relationships involves opposites attracting to a separate but connected balance. This means that when you love your self like God loves you, you bring a powerful presence designed to provide freedom and confidence.

Chapter 6

Relationship Opposites
Do Attract

*We must accept that this creative pulse within us is
God's creative pulse itself.*
—*Joseph Chilton Pearce, Child Development Professor*

Creation is designed with ebb and flow, seasons and cycles, ups and downs. Whether it is lunar cycles or the four distinct seasons in Midwest United States, there is a rhythm to life that affects you. The Bible reflects these same rhythms. It contains God's commands and his invitations, his condemnation and his forgiveness. God's word has a cadence that Christians learn to walk by and trust.

Relationships themselves experience these same rhythms. In the same way opposite magnetic poles attract, relationships tend to attract opposite traits. Partners in a marriage may find one a spender and one a saver. These differences between two people are the intended design that sparks energy to keep the relationship attractive. The habits and perspectives of someone else from a totally different viewpoint may interest or repel us – but they almost always spark some response.

This truth is clearly illustrated in male-female differences, but it is found in creation in everything from activity within the matching pairs of chromosome that make up our body, to mysterious, pulsing quasars light years away. It is literally found everywhere. Quasars, one of the brightest astronomical events in the galaxy, exist in relationship with the darkest of astronomical elements, something called, super-massive black holes. Paradoxically, some of the brightest elements known in the galaxy are in relationship with the darkest elements. It's an astronomical example of how opposites attract. Relationships – complimentary relationships seems to form the balance and tension present at the center of a healthy marriage, or at the center of the Milky Way.

The *image of God* mirrors relationships designed to complement one another, in others words, make one another whole. This is what theologians identify as "The Image of God." It reflects the intimate and intricate connection between God and humanity. It is the origin of the powerful nature of complementary relationships present everywhere.

So, from the beginning, relationship exists. In Genesis 1.26 it says, "*Let us make mankind...*" In these few words the faintest images and mysteries of relationship emerge. The fact that God was always in relationship (as odd as that sounds) seems to illustrate how relationships were and are everywhere all the time. What's been discovered from many scientific fields, including the relatively new quantum theory is this. *Relationships aren't something, they're everything.*

God, already in relationship with himself, creates and adds relationships outside himself with creation. The image of God is arguably the greatest and most mysterious gift of relationship itself. It produces an odd-sounding truth. God, who is three-in-one, creates you in his image. His image is defined as two people, male and female. Relationships define God's life with himself, his life with you, and your life with others.

The profound delight of this Biblical image is that it has an interesting impact on human relationships as well. The gift of complementary relationship is impressed on humanity by virtue of the creation of male and female. The nature of marriage is rooted in this truth. In a marriage, there are two (people) who reflect the image of the One (God). (Genesis 1.26f; Mark 10.8) Each is connected to the opposite complementary gender by relationship.

From the beginning, relationships produced life as part of God's grand design. Life itself was conceived within the relationship of God who initiated it all. (Genesis 1.26) In a similar way, this relational, creative God provides each gender the gift of one union to produce a new relationship. Their loving relationship, illustrated in complementary unity with the gift of sexuality (*"one flesh"* of Mark 19.5) creates a child. Now, the child becomes the genetic embodiment of the two genders who contribute to the one person. In this way, the gift of God is not only from participating in the creation of life, but also by giving the gift of another new relationship. Anyone who has had children instantly knows the huge impact this new relationship has on everyone else. All the relationships in the house shift when a new life comes home.

The *Image of God* is the "birthplace" of complementary relationship. Relationships are operating behind the scenes, like a universal computer code, in friendships, businesses, families or corporations

Relationships aren't something, they're everything. The *Imago Dei*, the image of God illustrates these very basic core truths I've nicknamed the universal operating system. From the beginning,

Relationships are a part of the very essence of God.

Relationships have always been around.

Complementary relationships (opposites attracting) produce energy to continue in relationship.

Relationships produce life.

Relationships aren't something, they're everything.

What does this mean?

The mysterious Christian doctrine of the Trinity states there is one God, yet three Persons. Each Person is different, but each person is in unity as One. So, even before everything began, attracting relationship existed. When God created humanity, he also established opposite attracting relationships. This truth illustrates the timelessness and lasting importance of relationships attracting opposite traits.

What can you do?

Thank God. Be you. Seek out diversity. Relationships of very different people can interact to form a unity of Spirit. Welcome diverse dialogue. Converse with people of widely different opinions. All of these things encourage one another and reflect the nature of God's design. These are usually life giving instead of life-draining connections. It improves your vision of the world when you see everything through the lens of interwoven and diverse relationships.

Chapter 7

Relationships Are Separate but Connected

ড়৸৶

"God is not solitude, but perfect communion."
— Pope Benedict XVI

T he mysterious three-in-one nature of the Trinity illustrates how relationship opposites attract. It provides the blueprint for healthy relationships today. As the Trinity has three persons, separate, yet connected, so our healthiest relationships are separate people connected. *Separate but connected* is a combination found in healthy relationships everywhere. It could describe the cells in your body, or be a description of a great friendship. Separate, but connected relationships are the healthiest.

From the beginning there is unity in diversity, oneness found in separateness. This paradox plays out throughout the Bible, history and anywhere with anyone. The Gospel of John records an intimate prayer between Jesus and his Father that demonstrates this same separate but connected relationship within God himself. It has been called Jesus' High Priestly prayer because within it Jesus intercedes for us in the same way a priest intercedes for the people in his care. It is found in John 17. Throughout the prayer, Jesus' conversation with his Father provides insight into their independent natures and also the intricate and intimate relationship that binds them together as One God. Frankly the entire prayer has to be read slowly to distinguish carefully between all the pronouns and references to the weave of relationships between God the Father and Jesus and between those two and you. Consider this one brief verse as a sampling of Jesus' elegant and passionate prayer. Jesus says,

> *"I do not ask for these only, but also for those who will believe in me through their word that they may all be one, just as you, father are in me, and I in you, that they also may be in us.... I in them and you in me. May they be brought to complete unity to let the world know that you sent me and have loved them even as you have loved me."* (John 17.20-23)

Throughout this prayer Jesus speaks of his separate but connected relationship with his Father. He converses with his Dad about weaving you into this same sacred relationship. Likewise healthy community finds its most mature expression when individuals have a clear, well-defined separateness to bring to the community. The healthier the individuals are in the family or group, the better the group functions. *Life is designed to be separate yet connected.*

This separate but connected balance continues to influence you over your lifetime. In the same way vows affect a marriage till death parts you, so striking life's separate but connected balance influences who you are and what you do – for a lifetime. Vows are more than some historical promise made, they shape a person, provide boundaries, and connect a spouse even while a spouse remains a separate individual. This is true if you're a single person as well. You're a son or daughter. It has been a relationship shaping you, and you shaping your mom/dad. Even when you were as tiny as seed, the relationship you had with your mom was changing her body chemistry, mood and decisions. Her relationship with your dad influenced her for better or worse which in turn influenced you, even though you were still intrauterine and a few millimeters long!

So, in the same way, the image in which you were created is not a one-time event like a marriage vow or a birth. Being created in the image of God is a continuing relationship that both creates and continues to re-create you in that image through your relationship with Jesus. The *Image of God* is what happens *as* you are in the presence of God. His divine image encompasses you and alters you through that sacred relationship. The *Image of God* is realized as you are connected to God even while you remain a separate child of God. The image of God is best reflected in you when you are an individual separate from God and connected to him.

Healthy relational spiritual life means being connected to the Father by his invitation through Jesus. It means that your spiritual self, though independent in your free will, also desires to stay connected to God to live in his image. When there is no relationship with God, there is no life, no image of his likeness or reflection of him in your life. The gospel becomes the story of reconnection. Jesus reestablishes the proper balance between you and God. Jesus exemplifies this relationship as he lives out the separate but connected balance on earth and ultimately pays the ultimate price to restore it.

You are invited by God to grow in his image as the Holy Spirit enables by continuing in relationship with him. The divine image is restored as you come to desire what blesses you and glorifies God. The healthiest balance is a lifestyle of taking care to nurture your self in order to connect with others. This balanced "separate but connected" tension is found in the Trinity, exercised between Jesus and his Father and finally given back to you after Jesus pays the price to have it restored. Indeed, the very definition of "God is love" (1 John 4.8) indicates that God is by nature relational. Love can only be expressed to another. By definition love requires relationship to be expressed.

What does this mean?

Healthy relationships are separate, but connected, as the Persons of the Trinity, Father, Son and Holy Spirit are separate, but connected. Their relationship sets the standard for your relationships. It is also reflected in the person of Jesus and his relationship to the Father. From the life of billions of cells living in your body, to the nature of healthy friendships and marriages, separate but connected living is God's grand design. These are relationships close enough to interact, but far enough apart to be independent.

What can you do?

Enter relationships with a separate but connected balance in mind. Observe relationships to see what happens when people take time for themselves (separate) in order to be with others (connected). Watch what happens to yourself and others when there is too much separateness (selfishness) or when the pendulum swings the other way and people take care of others to the point of being exhausted or resentful (over connecting). Look for the separate but connected relationship balance *everywhere*.

Chapter 8

Love Your Neighbor As Yourself

"Love your neighbor instead of yourself."
— What Many People Hear Jesus Say

Key to *The Love Paradox* is Jesus' response to the "ortho-doxy" of his day. Because Jesus' teachings of freedom began to loosen the grip of control the leaders of the day were exercising, they put together a politically odd group of church leaders who were out to test him. The original language, Greek, actually reads *"test him"* as a participle. So, it could be more lit-erally read, "to keep on testing him." The challenging question posed was *"Teacher, which command in God's law is most important?"* (Matthew 22.36 The Message)

Jesus responded with a quote from the Pentateuch, a name given to the first five books of the Bible, implying that his answer was anchored in their own teachings. Perhaps Jesus was illus-trating the answer was itself, timeless. Jesus' answer is a quote from Deuteronomy 6.5. It reads, *"Love the Lord your God with all your heart, with all your soul and all your mind. This is the first and greatest commandment."* (Matthew 22. 37,38) Without prompting, Jesus volunteers, *"And the second is like it, love your neighbor as yourself." All the law and prophets hang on these two commandments."* (Matthew 22. 39,40) This second response also comes from Leviticus 19.18

"Do not seek revenge or bear a grudge against one of your people, but love your neighbor as yourself. I am the LORD" It is here that Jesus places the two statements together much like combining ingredients in a recipe.

The greatest and the first thing to do is love God without holding back. The second, however, is integrated into the first – loving your neighbor *as yourself.* The most important element for such sacred behavior, such as loving your neighbor, is a loving relationship with your self. Note the interrelationship of love for God, neighbor and self. Jesus' summary integrates ancient Hebrew texts, life with God, community and relationships with your self.

Do you love your self?

Most people I ask recoil slightly from the question's impact, as though I had just asked something embarrassing. Do you sneak chocolate when no one is looking? Are you afraid to make left hand turns at busy intersections? Do you love your self? Most people seem to have the same curious and slightly self-conscious response. At best it assumes a misunderstanding, and at worst it may sound like a question meant to elicit guilt. When I ask this question in workshops I get a "Do I what?" kind of look. Eyes narrow, heads tilt and people mumble questions about why I want to know. Many are quickly trying to figure out if they're *supposed* to say yes…or no!

For most people, the call to passionately love God is easily understood, even if not practiced. Loving one's neighbor is easily enough understood, even if it's not practiced either. But, the standard against which one measures commitment to the same neighbor is all too easily dismissed. It's as though the last word of Jesus' great summary statement gets lost in translation. "Love your neighbor as *yourself.*" (Matthew 22.40 *emphasis added because most people need it added.*)

For many, most of the time, it's as though Jesus said, love your neighbor *instead of* yourself. There just seems to be something more culturally Christian acceptable than to say out loud,

"I love my self." Are you afraid to do it? Is it that you don't understand the question? Do you understand the question, but are afraid to reveal the self*ishness* with which you're so familiar? There are other occasions when the Bible uses a *Biblical love of self* as a standard to engage in relationship with others. In fact, *a Biblical love of self* is necessary *in order to* participate fully in all relationships and any community.

So, why the sheepish minority of raised hands at workshops when asked, "Who here can say they love themselves?" What is the hesitation that resists this – even though it is found at the core of Jesus' summary? Here are three possibilities.

The first response to run from a *love of self* confession might be from a confusion between *Biblical love of self* (the Bible's clear call) and self*ish* love (the Bible's clear warning), as contrasted in chapter five. In the movie *The Devil's Advocate* Al Pacino plays a shrewd and powerful lawyer who is the devil incarnate.[3] In the closing monologue, he dramatically identifies self*ish* love as "the all natural opiate of the masses." The New Testament identifies the works of the sinful nature with lists of behaviors that would qualify as such an opiate. Here's quotes from Jesus and St. Paul.

"What comes out of a man is what makes him 'unclean.' For from within, out of men's hearts, come evil thoughts, sexual immorality, theft, murder, adultery, greed, malice, deceit, lewdness, envy, slander, arrogance and folly. All these evils come from inside and make a man 'unclean.'" - Jesus (Matthew 7.20-23)

"The acts of the sinful nature are obvious: sexual immorality, impurity and debauchery, idolatry and witchcraft; hatred, discord, jealousy, fits of rage, selfish ambition, dissensions, factions and envy; drunkenness, orgies, and the like. I warn you, as I did before, that those who live like this will not inherit the kingdom of God. – St. Paul (Galatians 5.19-21)

When a *Biblical love of self* is mistaken for gratifying your impulses for pleasure, it is understandable why you might shy away from saying "I love myself." It is likely, however, you are not as practiced at recognizing appropriate, Biblical forms of love that bless, rather than curse. It's my guess you don't often attribute a *Biblical love of self* as something God is calling you to live and practice.

Secondly, Christians may be tentative about confessing a *Biblical love of self* because of a misunderstanding of the role of a Christian servant. Jesus' repeated call to pick up your cross and follow him sounds like it should eliminate any kind of love of self. The question arises, "How can I take up my cross and follow him – and – be loving of self at the same time?

Jesus gospel invitation is this, *"If anyone would come after me, let him deny himself and take up his cross and follow me."* (Matthew 10.38, Luke 14.27) The verb, "to follow," or "would come after me" is in the present tense, inferring an ongoing process as opposed to a one time event. Expanded it might read, "If you're going to spend a lifetime time following me…" It implies commitment, duration and purpose. So if Jesus is going to define your lifestyle, you must be equipped to say no to yourself when tempted to take the short cut. This intentional sacrificial lifestyle is your personal version of taking up your cross to follow Jesus.

Perhaps you think that picking up your cross and following Jesus is running yourself ragged. It's just as clearly wrong, but it has the unfortunate element of looking better around religious people. Following this kind of call to pick up your cross and follow him leads to burn out or break down. In this line of thinking, following Jesus amounts to working to exhaustion, or so the religious sounding thought goes through your head. Rather than being a good steward of your limited physical, emotional and spiritual energy, you may be working without appropriate renewal, and calling it taking up your cross and following Jesus.

In reality, it's actually destroying self and hindering the mission. For those who are trying to look religious, a *Biblical love of self* is thought of as an ideal out of reach, rather than God's good idea. Ironically, such nonsense, although dressed up as loving behavior, is likely part of the excuse that keeps people from pursuing the hard work of loving.

The invisible connection Jesus illustrated between the top two commandments when he said, "*and the second is like it. Love your neighbor as yourself*" is the point. Tying these two together distinguishes between *love of self* as the Bible's call, and self*ish* love with the Bible's warning. It clarifies how daily picking up your cross does indeed amount to following Jesus faithfully. It is more effective with an appropriate stewardship of self. It will place a strong focus on management of self in order to lead others. Rather than a new technique per se, it is a focus on self for the purpose of leading others and promoting greater emotional and spiritual health in community. The call to pick up one's cross and follow Jesus is an invitation for a Biblical love of self in order to more fully love others. People who don't take spiritual and emotional short cuts are that much stronger when it comes time to face life's challenges.

The delight of *The Love Paradox* is that once you're given the Gift, the gift of this Biblical love of self, you are then supplied the vigor to love the Lord your God with everything you are. You can then enjoy a *Biblical love of self* that connects you to your neighbor, or your soccer teammates, or your work group, or your wife, husband, kids or grouchy person at the grocery store. In this way, Jesus teaches you to manage yourself well *for the sake of the mission.*

He calls and equips you to love and care for yourself, in order to love and care for others because you have been loved and cared for by him first.

What does this mean?

A Biblical love of self is necessary in order to have a Godly love for others. Oddly enough, harmonious relationships require a love and acceptance of self in the same way God has loved and accepted you first. You can't hate yourself and love your neighbor. Your love will be experienced as shallow – perhaps even manipulative. Ultimately, hating yourself can destroy both your self and your neighbor. Loving yourself as God has loved you enhances both.

What can you do?

Accept the forgiving gift of God in Jesus so you may love yourself in order to love your neighbor and thereby love the Lord, your God with all you are. In this way you can avoid both extremes of self-loathing and self-centeredness. Curiously enough, a Biblical love of self is centered in the love of God – not you. It too is a part of the love paradox. Yet, it allows for you to love others deeply, in part because you can do so freely without using them to meet your own needs.

Chapter 9

Presence Just Is
(It Is Just Amazing)

"My presence will go with you..."
—*God, to an Anxious Moses*

The powerful active ingredient in relationship is presence.
If the relationship of the Trinity as one God, three persons is mysterious, the Presence of God is amazingly mysterious. If Jesus as true God and true man is perplexing, then the Presence of God in Jesus is amazingly perplexing. It is the presence of God that so powerfully connects us to the love of self, neighbor and ultimately to God himself. According to the Bible, the Presence of God organizes, orders and integrates. It accompanies, partners, challenges, changes and alters. Paradoxically, it comforts and assures when present and frightens and alarms when seemingly absent. It is tangible, but difficult to define. It is invisible yet discernible. It is everywhere and right here, right now. It is in water and the Word, bread and wine, Body and Blood. It is within your grasp and yet beyond your reach. It gives life. It is life. It is the heart of *agape* love. It is Jesus.

In the beginning, the Presence of God was, well, present. Genesis 1.2, *"...the Spirit of God was hovering over the waters."* The mystery begins early. *The Spirit*, which could be translated from the original Hebrew as *breath* or *wind of God* is a life-giving and invisible moving force of this presence. From the nature of this mystery flows what this *Spirit, breath, or wind of God* does. The Spirit *hovers.*

All this illustrates the power in God's Presence by simply yet powerfully, *being there.* When the Spirit shows up, life comes into existence. Order and orderliness, boundaries and definition, all begin to emerge from this Presence. Interconnection and inter-dependence are formed by his Presence. Higher complexities materialize and each becomes a part of the whole because of this Presence. The power of Presence creates, unites and integrates your life.

From the story of the Fall of Adam and Eve, you see the widespread effects of the absence of God's presence. There is destruction for the serpent, pain for the mom, futility for the breadwinner as well as shame and guilt for the fleeing couple. Eve and Adam, aware that their self*ish* act is a destruction of trust, run from God's Presence. Immediately, you see visible and immediate consequences of separating from God's Presence. (Genesis 3)

Later, their son, Cain, felt the agonizing absence of God's Presence. After he murdered his brother, Abel, Cain is horrified and distressed at being cast outside of God's Presence.

> *"Today you are driving me from the land, and I will be hidden from your presence; I will be a restless wanderer on the earth, and whoever finds me will kill me."* (Genesis 4.14)

From early on in ancient history, we learn what happens out-side of the Presence of God. Restless wandering in fear fuels Cain's apprehension. It's likely descriptive of all of humanity at one time or another. Aimlessness and lack of purpose, lack of direction and meaningless lives might well describe the essence of many anxieties.

Cain is banished to the Land of Nod. In the Land of Nod (the Hebrew word means *wandering*), there is no order and predictable patterns on which to build. Dinner can happen at any time. You can eat in your room if you want. The TV can be playing reruns in the background. You don't have to do your homework, nor mature in your spirit. Accountability is sacrificed to convenience. Family traditions are optional. Computer games with ear buds are everywhere. It's important to work overtime for the money, and then not have the time to have company over for dinner. Relationships randomly happen and don't need to be nurtured with precious time. You never have enough hours in the day, and symptom relief is more important than working the mission. In the Land of Nod, that which was integrated, dis-integrates; that which had order becomes dis-orderly; that which had rich meaning becomes meaning-less.

The Presence of God dissipates the land of Nod like the illusory mirage of an oasis in the desert disappears as you draw closer. Like a desert illusion, it only looks good from a distance. You want it to be there, but the truth is you've conjured it up in your thirsty mind. All of the *wandering in life,* "Nodding off," (if you will), is dissipated in the Presence of God where mission and purpose, relationship and partnership are the results of God showing up. God's Presence transforms a spiritual nomadic life into a lifestyle of focused mission and purpose.

Still, the whole concept of God's presence can be elusive and tricky to define – that is until Jesus shows up. Then, suddenly, mysterious Presence moves into the neighborhood.

"The Word became flesh and made his dwelling among us. We have seen his glory, the glory of the One and Only, who came from the Father, full of grace and truth." (John 1.14)

"For God was pleased to have all his fullness dwell in him..." (Colossians 1.19)

"For in Christ all the fullness of the Deity lives in bodily form." (Colossians 2.9)

Jesus does away with the mysterious characteristics of presence wrapped in the ambiguous shroud of spirituality. In its place is someone living down the street asking to come to your house for dinner. He's bringing Bread and Wine, challenge, comfort, Truth and hope. It's okay; he knocks first and waits for you to invite him in. You don't have to worry about picking up the place or vacuuming straight lines in the carpet – he's come looking for you and the mess you are. He appreciates that lived-in look!

It's okay; the Presence of God won't look scary like the aliens from Area 51. He doesn't resemble the North Wind character from cartoons. He'll not tell your secrets out loud or ask if you've been naughty or nice. He looks very ordinary, seems a bit underdressed and might need a haircut. Is it possible for the Presence of God to be this disarming?

Be courageous if you answer the door because it takes courage to be this vulnerable. He will look you straight in the eyes, bring all the Presence of God to bear, and love you. Be careful, because it's his *agape* love - and this stuff will kill you and then rebirth a *new* you. This is what happens because he's full of grace and truth and the fullness and presence of God speaks and acts through him. (John 1.14)

This Presence of God has been witnessed across time and throughout history. The Presence of God has been illustrated in fires that don't consume in the burning bush of Moses' encounter (Exodus 3) and three guys named Shadrach, Meshach and Abednego. (Daniel 3.20*f*) Daniel also records an odd sort of incident that is still a cliché today about reading the *"handwriting on the wall."* God's presence delivers a clear message to the King that only Daniel can interpret. This presence was in the Tongues of Fire over the heads of the multi-linguistic disciples in Acts 2. God's Presence was a Pillar of Fire leading stubborn followers through difficult wilderness circumstances (Exodus 13.21). At the dedication of Tabernacle worship in the dessert, *"the glory of the Lord"* filled the tent. (Leviticus 9) The prophet Ezekiel observed it in a vision as mysterious as it is detailed. (Ezekiel 10, 43, 44)

This Presence of God always affects something, changes someone and accomplishes his purpose throughout history. At a time when Moses was having one of those end-of-his-rope days, God told him, *"My Presence will go with you, and I will give you rest."* *(Exodus 33.14)* Moses didn't ask for the texts on wilderness leadership, nor receive from God a six part worship series on dealing with stiff-necked people. What he got was God's company, his promise to journey with him - and this would give him rest.

King David had eight wives, but still found time to wonder, then wander. After committing adultery with Bathsheba and murdering her husband, the prophet Nathan convicts David. (2 Samuel 11*f*) In a fear reminiscent of Cain's, David cries out, *"Do not cast me from your presence or take your Holy Spirit from me."* (Psalm 51.11) Like Cain before him, like those who have been placed before a spouse confessing a betrayal of marital trust, the relationship lost is what causes wandering. King David who had a history of dancing in the presence of the Lord, now faces his greatest fear of losing the relationship that had so faithfully been with him through years of facing giants, ducking spears and being on the run. The relationship with God isn't something – it is everything to King David.

There are many, many Psalms that define and describe the power of God's presence. For example, Psalm 16.11, *"You have made known to me the path of life; you will fill me with joy in your presence."* Note the connection between purpose, relationship and joy. The Hebrew word for *"joy"* is in the plural. This happens only one other time in Psalm 45, so it is apparent the author is experiencing and expressing *abundant* joy, or *overwhelming* joy, or *lots and lots of* what he chooses to define as plural joy provided by God's Presence!

Reflecting on this passage reminded me of an adoption I witnessed. I was invited to the airport (at a time when non-passengers could wait at the gate) and, with a host of family and friends, awaited an infant girl from overseas. Balloons, banners, streamers, and giddy enthusiasm marked the anticipation of the infant's arrival. It was contagious to those waiting for their flight. When the parents actually saw the face of the infant in the arms of the traveling caretaker, there were tears of joy and a flush of emotion that spilled out and over all of us throughout the entire wing of the terminal. The parents, of course, were overflowing with delighted emotion. This was also true, of course, of gathered family and friends. But there was also joy spilling over to those waiting for the next flight. One lady said out loud, speaking to no one in particular, "I'm so glad I got to be a part of this." As a result of the presence of God in this place, her joy was what the psalmist might call joy in the plural. John, apparently one of Jesus closest friends, seals the connection between joy in the plural and truth in the Presence of God. He writes *"This then is how we know that we belong to the truth, and how we set our hearts at rest in his presence."* (1 John 3.19)

Things dramatically change in the face of the Presence of God. Community becomes a deeper communion. *Just face it.* The phrase itself calls us to turn toward the issue. *Look at me when I'm talking to you.* This one, perhaps most familiar to parents, calls for rolling eyes to turn toward the instructions to assure the message is getting through. In court, you're given the opportunity to *face your accusers.* When emails just won't communicate the nuances you're trying to get across, you'll travel for a *face-to-face* meeting to gather important language unavailable in impersonal emails (no matter how many "emoticons" you include).

A global company my youngest son Dave worked for spends millions each year sending its executives around the world for *face to face* contacts even though they have the technology to link up in myriad other video forms. They, like many businesses, understand the cost-benefit ratio of *face-to-face* gatherings.

Why all this digression about the face? Each of these examples, and many more are but testimony to the nature of presence – expressed in the action of *turning your face toward.* There is something more at work than the latest business deal or parental admonishment. These are all rooted in the connection between presence and turning your face toward someone – either physically or emotionally. Oddly enough, there is ancient truth involved in showing your face to someone. Consider that from both the original Old Testament Hebrew, and New Testament Greek, the New International Version, and many other versions usually translate *"face"* as *"presence"*.

When Cain was banished – he objected because he would not see the face of God any longer. When King David confessed his adultery, he was frightened he wouldn't see God's face as a result of his lusts. Those imprisoned, and those left behind, long to see each other face-to-face again. Those imprisoned receive further punishment by being isolated from anyone's face. Ultimately, isolation accompanied by sensory deprivation where prisoners are deprived of sensory input through muffs, goggles, gloves and the like, creates an enormous psychological impact that includes hallucinations and psychological breakdowns. Face it, we're not only created to be *face to face,* but we are also designed to be connected through our senses. When that connection is denied, for whatever reason, there is great angst, great pain and even psychological breakdown.

There is plural joy in presence. There is great pain without it. After his face-to-face encounter with God to receive the Ten Commandments, Moses had a face radiant from God's presence. (Exodus 34.29*f*) The presence of a beloved's face stirs passion. The absence of a loved one's face brings longing. Perhaps this is why the Bible says *"Look to the LORD and his strength; seek his face always."* (Psalm 105.4) Something profound happens in God's presence, and you become different after the experience. You're rearranged, emotionally touched, spiritually moved or altered somehow.

This is what makes presence so amazing. It organizes, orders and integrates the universe itself. It accompanies, provides company and partnership for humanity, and for you, personally. It challenges, changes and alters as you are engaged. It is comforting and assuring when present – to the point of plural joy. It is frightening and alarming when felt absent – to the point of disturbing anxiety. It is tangible, but difficult to define – like a thought conjuring up a memory. It is invisible yet discernible, like an intimate connection with a beloved. It is everywhere, and especially right here, right now. It is both universal and personal. It is within our grasp and beyond our reach like a prayer ascending. It gives life by being there. It is life all by itself. It is the heart of *agape* love. It is Jesus.

A long time ago God wanted to let his people know he was present – that his Presence was with them. He wanted you to know through daily routines and relationships, that he was for you, *facing* life and death alongside you. He told Moses to tell Aaron and the priests to give this blessing, recorded in Numbers 6.24-26. It is still used today to assure of the Presence of God.

The Lord bless you and keep you.
The Lord make his face shine upon you and be gracious to you.
The Lord turn his face toward you and give you peace.

What does this mean?

The powerful active ingredient in relationship is presence. When God's Presence is present, big things happen. In its absence lies the destruction of isolation and the pain of separation. Healthy relationships bring the amazing Presence of God to bear within them for big things to happen. The sense of attention and focus you bring to a relationship brings your presence to bear and directly impacts the other person.

What can you do?

Be present. Stop multitasking when interacting with others. Place your smart phone on silence, put it in your pocket and enjoy a face-to-face meal. Be attentive during interactions to reduce miscommunication and enhance heart to heart contact. Build in regular opportunity to experience the presence of God in your life. Experiencing God in worship, in communion, in creation, in prayer and spiritual disciplines cultivates and matures your soul. This in turn allows others, especially those in intimate relationships, to experience God through you.

Things Change When You Show Up

Don't you hate it when you walk into the room and sense an awkward silence? You can't tell if they were talking about you or just talking about something they didn't want you to know about, but your presence changed the atmosphere of the room.

You just returned to work from sick leave to discover people have decorated the office with welcome banners and get well wishes. In different ways people keep saying how much they missed you, how they're glad you're back and how great it is to see you. People's workday is different because you've recovered and returned to work.

The shooting guard on your college basketball team can't seem to miss a shot. Almost everything she throws up at the whoop goes in. She's got energy, and more drive than you've ever seen. She's playing a mean defensive game and has a couple of steals by half time. When congratulated and questioned during a time out, she says, "My Dad drove for eight hours and is here to see me play for the first time." Everyone jokes about bringing him to every succeeding game. Her Dad's presence at the game provided inspiration for her game.

The presence of one person has unquestionable and pro-found impact on a room, a work place, a team – or a culture. This section examines the powerful impact of your presence and encourages you to show up.

Chapter 10

Your Transformation Transforms Others

৩৯১

"Leadership, often thought to be about action, is more about interaction…"
—Peter Steinke

B ecause the power of presence is amazing, the presence of a leader is powerful and effective. Any leader has primary responsibility to manage life's tension and balances well because the leader's presence has a direct impact on the group or organization. In large part this means practicing God's design as separate but connected to those you serve. In this way you will illustrate how leaders are responsible for their position in the family/organization – instead of trying to control it all. In this way you will fundamentally influence the organization while you manage yourself well through the process. Essentially, when it's done right, both the individual leader and the group as a whole win!

Leaders, dads and moms with high chairs, or business people in board chairs are called on to first receive the offered gift of *agape* love and then take care of the gift received. It means Dad is making time for relationship with God through worship and devotion to strengthen his inner spirit. He's setting aside time for the disciplines of exercise and diet to minimize destructive impulses. It means dad is investing either in bread winning or bread making for the sake of the family, so there is real evidence of relationship connection. It flows to wife/mom in the form of a bond so strong he would take a bullet for her.

Issues of balance and health are so important because they promote the Creator's balances. It is the responsibility of the leader to understand the connectivity of creation, the powerful presence of the face of God and then be that connected presence. In turn, this will provide order to lead others to experience things needed for their souls, such as rest and (even plural) joy. It is also the responsibility of the leader to reflect the same presence of God so that others might experience adventurous times – and still know of rest and joy in the midst of it.

Your calling might be to lead a family or a corporation on explorations and risky journeys and still do it with a sense of peace that passes understanding. It could be like the call of God given to Moses to overcome a super power, lead thousands through a desert and overcome an occupied land. (Exodus 3) It is the challenge to tell everyone, everywhere, everything that Jesus taught – that the whole world might be saved. (Matthew 28.19f) Being a steward of your position of leadership will allow you to maturely manage the anxiety that naturally rises within yourself and automatically flows throughout your home or work place when things begin to change.

Leaders are called on to be a step-down transformer of people's anxieties. This is important in order to reduce the apprehensions of the immature that longs for symptom relief from the discomfort of change. This is more important than ever as people become accustomed to quick fixes and seek the anxiety-numbing opiates of the day. The position of leadership in the system will be separate enough to see everything working clearly, yet close enough to calm those reacting with a herd mentality that wants to stampede at the first sniff of difficulty.

The leader encourages the necessary changes, leads through the difficult or exciting places, and manages self in order to move forward, alleviating anxiety along the way. It is during anxious times that the responsibility of the leader to be the presence of God is most challenged. Anxiety and fear are ever-present and everywhere. Watch any twenty-four hour news station. It is present in our schools and courts as illustrated by anxious children and litigious parents. The challenges to careful self-management are everywhere.

The more tense things become the more important it is to first manage your self well. The part I discovered I like most is that this is God's freeing gift. It works like this. A healthy marriage is separate but connected. This two-but-one marriage produces an appropriately balanced emotional atmosphere that fosters a healthy environment in which to raise children. Children experience the presence of balance in the marriage and are able to better understand and respect boundaries in other areas of life. Bring your family to the school classroom or the company picnic and watch how people observe and sense the power of your relationships working as they experience healthy interactions. Usually people aren't aware they're experiencing anything other than people that are a joy to be around.

This integrated design of creation means the best way to transform another is to be transformed yourself. It means that in order to be a good father you try to live out being a good son. It means that bringing health to a marriage as a wife is connected to being a good daughter. Captains of teams will provide inspiration for teammates by being physically and emotionally prepared for the contest first. There is great joy in this strength that builds up from the inside and then moves outward. There is great delight in this freedom that allows influence of others to come from the work you're doing on yourself. There is great relief from feeling the pressure to manipulate others when you can accomplish more by changing yourself. This is the good stuff.

There's no question of the necessity to know the material of your trade. It's still critically important to work the disciplines of your field; to study hard the content of your career, to know the information about soccer or short sales. This isn't about taking short cuts or avoiding the hard work of knowing your muscle groups as a physical therapist, or an accountant forgetting about tax codes. However, beyond the popular axiom, "Information is power" I have come to discover that knowing myself is *more* powerful and that ultimately, having a Biblical love for myself *is even more powerful* still.

The strength of this power is found in its ability to transform in meaningful and lasting ways. Informational power comes because information is always changing, so there is always need for more updated data. Appropriate stewardship of self is powerful because it encourages lasting change from within that influence those around you. Because of the unchanging design of creation, when you respond differently, people respond differently to you. A new interaction births a new relationship – even if it occurs in subtle ways or small degrees. B*eing the change* you want to see has far more impact than describing change in a Power Point presentation.

You're naturally drawn to leaders who *are* loving more than leaders who describe what it means to love. People speak of charisma in others to describe how charismatic leaders make *you* feel to explain how or why you follow the people you do. The cliché "people don't care how much you know until they know how much you care" rings true because your transformation transforms others.

Key words such as authentic, genuine and real are used in the marketplace to describe beer, cars, even dips for chips. Those who work hard to sell you stuff work hard to know what triggers some of your most basic impulses and desires. What they've learned in their research is how to touch something deeply within the consumer and then attempt to attach a basic human desire to their product.

The gift of *The Love Paradox* is that it inspires confidence in your self to which Jesus attaches *the mission*. This in turn is mutually reinforcing. When you are working God's mission, be it forgiving a friend or taking the kids to baseball practice, your personal stewardship of self, enhances your ability to connect to the lives of others. If you will not forgive yourself, your forgiveness to others can be received as shallow. If you have not set aside the time for your marriage, your kid's activities will be diminished when mom and dad sit awkwardly in different bleachers trying to pretend everything is normal.

The delight of the gift is the relief from exhaustion. The joy of this renewed strength is in first *receiving* the gift of *agape* love and then being a steward of the love received – within your own soul. The first call of this stewardship is to love God back – wholly, comprehensively, with all that you can muster. However, it turns out God isn't in need of any favors or ministrations: he's good. So he says you can love him back by loving yourself *in order to* love your neighbor.

You must not take vengeance or bear a grudge against the children of your people, but you must love your neighbor as yourself. I am the Lord. (Leviticus 19.18)

The foreigner who resides with you must be to you like a native citizen among you; so you must love him as yourself, because you were foreigners in the land of Egypt. I am the Lord your God. (Leviticus 19.34)

But if you fulfill the royal law as expressed in this Scripture, "You shall love your neighbor as yourself," you are doing well. (James 2.8)

For the whole law can be summed up in a single commandment, namely, "You must love your neighbor as yourself. (Galatians 5.14)

For the commandments, "Do not commit adultery, do not murder, do not steal, do not covet," (and if there is any other commandment) are summed up in this, "Love your neighbor as yourself. (Romans 13.9)

These quotes regarding the connection between an appropriate love of self and the effect of that stewardship of self on others is echoed from Ghandi to Benjamin Franklin. Throughout history leaders of all sorts have understood the necessity to be transformed before transforming others. Consider:

"I wanted to change the world. But I have found that the only thing one can be sure of changing is oneself." - Aldous Huxley, British author of *"Brave New World"*

"Everyone thinks of changing the world, but no one thinks of changing himself." - - *Leo Nikolaevich Tolstoy*, Russian author of *"War and Peace"*

"When we are no longer able to change a situation - we are challenged to change ourselves.
–*Victor Frankl*, Austrian Neurologist, Psychologist and Holocaust survivor

"It is not love of self, but hatred of self which is at the root of troubles that affect our world."
– Eric Hoffer, 20th century American writer and philosopher

Self-love, in a well-regulated breast, is as the steward of the household, superintending the expenditure, and seeing that benevolence herself should be prudential, in order to be permanent, by providing that the reservoir which feeds should also be fed.
–Charles Caleb Colton, 19th century English cleric and writer

That man alone loves himself rightly who procures the greatest possible good to himself through the whole of his existence and so pursues pleasure as not to give for it more than it is worth. – Benjamin Franklin, 18th century American statesman

Your transformation will transform others anywhere, anytime or in any circumstance. This pattern is clearly defined over the last 3500 years or so, from the ancient text of Leviticus, to the inspiring pens of poets, leaders and philosophers, your best leadership influence is by being a great steward of who God has made you.

What does this mean?

The largest portion of leadership is stewardship of self. When you manage yourself well, whatever you have to say is "heard" more clearly. When there is poor management of self, like static on the radio, it interferes with whatever message you're trying to convey.

What can you do?

Begin within. From parents to presidents, whether leading children or employees, leadership influences others when it comes from integrity. If you know your business plan, but don't have a plan for your own personal growth, much of what you say and do will seem like words without conviction. Seek to be transformed before working on transforming others.

Chapter 11

Learning to Observe Relationships

ॐ

"Huh?"
— Michael Spehn, Author of The Color of Rain
(His response when I told him,
"Presence is systemically determinative.")

Presence is systemically determinative!
The only problem with this expression is that it's spoken in a language few speak – the jargon of social scientists and maybe a few stray biologists. It was actually a title to one of the chapters of my original doctoral dissertation that birthed *The Love Paradox*. It was written to impress the Review Committee full of Ph.D.'s. My wife, Marilouise remained unimpressed and when she read it simply said, "Speak English."

So, at her urging, I've set aside confusing jargon to make the key point of this chapter in English. I want you to see how creation is intimately and intricately connected by relationships of all sorts. As you learn to "see" relationships and the effect relationships have on others, you'll be pleasantly surprised at the education you receive. It's called, *systemic* thinking. Understanding the basics of *systemic thinking* changes your perspective and develops insights into the importance of healthy self-management and the amazing effect it has on one another.

Basically *systemic* thought is seeing the big picture. It is the perception of patterns, orbits, and interactions found everywhere. For example, systemic thinking is like viewing designs of the marching band from the top row of the stadium, rather than focusing binoculars on a single personality within the band. From the top of the bleachers you can clearly see the band members form the school letters. By contrast, from the vantage point close to the field, it looks like intersections of people stepping, turning and stomping to some invisible plan. It might even look like random motion. If you're in the band you concentrate on steps and turns per beat and measure, but have no vision to determine what the big picture looks like. You have to march with confidence that you're doing your part and everyone else in the band is marching to the same tune directed by the elevated leader.

When you're on the field marching, counting beats and steps, your personality isn't what makes the thing work. It's keeping count of your beats and steps and musician-by-musician managing the syncopation, rhythms and dance necessary from everyone to create the appropriate image for those in the stands. When you're in the seats down low, you are likely to have difficulty seeing the larger picture. This is true, in part, because you're close enough to see the tuba guy turning red, the drummer with the frown on his face and the slight trip of the flautist remembering a ninety-degree turn at the very last moment. Your viewpoint is more likely to see greater details in each person. This viewpoint, however, diminishes the larger picture perspective. There's a tendency to be captured by the color of the uniforms or an un-tucked shirt of the drum major and, therefore, miss the larger picture the band has rehearsed for months.

For those seated high above the field, there is enough perspective to see the big "F" (for University of Florida, an alma mater). The point is the big picture is revealed by a change of perspective. Learning to *think systemically* is learning to see order where people at eye level see randomness. Learning to *think systemically* is training your self to steer clear of the minutiae of the mundane and the distractions of the details in order to see the larger message. Learning to *think systemically* is both appreciative of all the hard work from the red-faced tuba player along with the ability to see the larger image for which he's worked so hard to be a part.

Systemic thinking is like a satellite view of a hurricane. From this perspective you are able to see the connection between a thunderstorm in Africa and a category three storm hundreds of miles in diameter coming ashore in your New Orleans neighborhood.

The basic pattern is this. A thunderstorm born in Africa is blown out to sea by the trade winds blowing from east to west. Over the warm waters near the equator the moisture rises, then cools and falls, increasing the storm's energy. As this continues, it begins to rotate pulling into itself more energy. The trade winds transport this whole process over days and thousands of warm ocean miles. This gives the storm both the time, and processes necessary to become more and more intense. When it arrives on US soil, it is not happy.

Thinking systemically understands there are many interactions necessary to generate huge emotional storms in your living room or on your work team. Storms in families rise up regularly and normally. However, when these seemingly minor storms are not taken seriously, they tend to be ignored. When this happens, this normal storm drifts outside the home into school, band, or the basketball camp. Over time it begins to spin larger and carry increasingly destructive forces with wider impact.

If your spouse rages at home, a systemic view is very helpful. It allows you to understand how hurricane strength emotional outbursts may be made up of small family storms that were never resolved. You may have to deal with the lightning strikes of anger over your head, but you realize this thing was whirling for a long time before it arrived on your shoreline.

It's not license to allow for continued inappropriate behavior. It is opportunity to make thoughtful decisions about whether to approach or remain separate enough for emotional, sometimes even physical safety. Because such events are not formed in a day, leaders of organizations or families will learn to develop systemic eyes (so to speak) and notice the nature of the relationships of people around you. Systemic thinking develops a type of radar tracking that allows for anticipation of potential problem interactions that might develop into future storms.

Thinking *systemically* provides opportunity for some objectivity in the middle of what otherwise might be a stormy encounter. Perhaps you've noticed your co-workers tense relationships. It may be you've seen how defensive your friend is to criticism. Maybe your teammate doesn't like to be coached through missed lay-ups on the basketball court. While observing the telltale relationships around this person through systemic eyes, you begin the see the systemic force field and are likely more prepared, or at least less surprised, by stormy outbursts.

Systemic eyes view the complex immune system response to a virus entering the body as "T" cells, "B" cells, antigens that trigger antibodies synchronize to eliminate the viral intruder. It is less about the runny nose the virus produces; the drippy nasal passages and the sneezing are outward and visible signs of a deeper more complex interaction. The body is responding *systemically* to the disease intruder. Those who study the immune system will tell you how the immune system learns and grows stronger through some exposure to bacteria and viruses. There is intricate interaction between these infectious agents and an immune system that learns to fight off these intruders and grows stronger from the process.

In fact, some in this field hold to thinking called "The Hygiene Hypothesis."[4] This research is examining the relationship between those who are not exposed to a wide range of these bacterial and viral challenges and as a result develop a less mature immune system. Many in the field of research pose a connection between an unchallenged immune system and allergies. In a passing conversation with a physician who specializes in immunology, she called these over-protected immune systems "bored."

She spoke of the autoimmune problems they cause when they go looking for trouble.

The "bored" immune system and the spiritually "bored" organization are not equipped for the trespassers that infect. *Systemic* eyes provide the insight to see why this happens. Mistakes and failures serve as spiritual antigens necessary to prepare for the next set of challenges. They are a helpful part of strengthening an immune system. Families who are adventurous and ready to forgive develop a resiliency that is able to overcome failures and heartache as a necessary part of life. Instead of living in fear that someone might get hurt, they live expectantly knowing that healing strengthens and prepares for the next adventure.

Systemic interaction is illustrated in family interplay on a white water rafting experience. The challenge of negotiating a river illustrates the complementary roles necessary to overcome complicated conditions through rapids. If you're on a class I float trip down a lazy river, the roles of each person in the boat are helpful but not critical to float to the end of your tour where guides pull you ashore and provide a picnic lunch. Under those relaxing conditions you'll still see roles for everyone, but they're somewhat interchangeable. If mom wants to change places in the raft to get a picture, some careful, even playful maneuvering can achieve the perfect frame without tipping everyone over.

Turn up the water volume intensity to an intermediate class III experience and the interaction in the boat becomes much more important. Narrow channels, critical maneuvering and quick responses to changing conditions highlight the need for everyone to interact well to stay dry and safe. In order to "draw" the boat sideways past an obstacle, complementary, even opposing paddle maneuvers may be necessary. The teamwork relationships are more than helpful; they are necessary for safe completion of the trip.

Take it up to the expert class V rapids ratings and someone's life may depend on the team relationships. Frequent obstacles, steep chutes and large waves demand outstanding skills. You must have calm thought under difficult conditions and strength of body and character in order to make it to a clearing to strike camp for the night.

The *systemic* illustrations are found in the interactions of rafters in any class rapid, but become increasingly obvious in rougher, faster waters. It is important for families to focus on cooperative interaction when life is easily flowing along at class I speeds. Balanced distribution, accommodating each other and interacting with the whole boat are all important. This interaction will be more than important as volume, speed, waves and obstacles increase. If one individual neglects personal strength, everyone else may suffer later. If one person panics, the lives of everyone may be endangered. Appropriate stewardship of self enhances the interactions and the mission is more likely to be accomplished. First, manage yourself well, in order to interact with everyone else well, in order to make it to shore later.

Lastly, consider how *systemic* interaction is exemplified in magnetic fields where two interactive magnetic sources form a magnetic *field* between them. The invisible, but powerful *field* is the product of their relationship and proximity to one another. Metal filings will dance as you move the magnets. It's the magnetic relationship that is determining the pattern of the dancing metal filings. It's not the personality of the metal filings that determine the intensity of the dance.

With the picture of metal filings being pulled and pushed around a magnetic field, consider a home with mom and dad arguing while the kids are in the room. Imagine they're arguing through a divorce and custody rights. The divorcing duo is creating an *emotional field* that is pulling and tugging at the kids. Who has not known of someone who has been pulled and tugged back and forth by disruptive, polarizing magnetic forces? Whether it's the polarities of divorcing parents or opposing camps in the workplace, systemic thinking supplies insight into why those caught in the middle are feeling the intensity of the pulling, pushing and abuse from embattled leaders.

At all times, and in all places, life is interconnected. As you learn to see and think systemically, you can watch interactions escalate or diminish based on yours and other's response. As you gain insights from systemic thinking, you will be able to decide how to respond, and far less likely to be caught up in reactive, escalating responses that diminish rather than foster relationship.

Perhaps you'll agree with me. Presence is systemically determinative!

What does this mean?

As invisible relationship connections become visible to you, it is like looking at a marching band from the top row of the stadium. You begin to see the patterns that make up life, not simply people in the band. You'll manage responsibilities with an understanding of how moving one band member affects the whole picture. By encouraging healthy interaction, you increase the likelihood of the success of the mission and the individual health of those on the mission.

What can you do?

Take a few steps back. Seeing the larger picture of what's going on requires a satellite's perspective. Stepping back from the emotional intensity of the moment and asking yourself what's going on allows a wider-angle lens perspective. Step back and note the way people are relating to one another. When you are a student of the way people treat and interact with each other you will discover how the interactions around you affect life.

Stay the Course and Stay Connected

"The history of liberty is a history of resistance."
—Woodrow T. Wilson

Whether you are a soccer coach or a political strategist, you can count on resistance to your goals ahead. If you are a pastor of a rural parish, or the president of General Motors, resistance to the objectives ahead is inevitable. If you are in a troubled marriage, single, or single again, there is interpersonal struggle for the relationship growth ahead.

This next section coaches you through this resistance - that is quite literally everywhere. You're invited to *stay the course and stay connected*. As you practice living out this balance you'll be able to lead your family or your rugby team through the maze of obstacles in front of you. No matter what, when or where – there are always obstacles to accomplishing your mission.

There is often great difficulty in the balance of staying the course and staying connected. It can be dangerous to live and love adventurously. Ask those who followed Columbus' discovery of new worlds with new worlds of their own. Discoveries by Galileo, Verrazano, Luther, Calvin and other reformers, were accompanied by risks, threats, sabotage – even people who didn't like them much anymore. Ed Friedman, in his book, *Failure of Nerve: Leadership in an Age of Quick Fix* does a wonderful job of illustrating the persevering nature of Renaissance leaders.[5] I recommend his book for a larger view of the impact adventurous leaders had on leading Europe from the Dark Ages into new worlds.

Like them, you too are in a constant state of overcoming obstacles. These obstacles might be one of a million concerns in parenting or career/professional struggles like working with the union as a foreman on the shop floor. One of the most significant perils you face in leading through any change is being unprepared for this inevitable resistance – especially your own internal resistance to meeting resistance. Either internal or external resistance can throw you off mission, but your own personal reluctance is likely the more invisible.

Chapter 12

Your Resistance
to Meeting Resistance

ॐ

"Change is hard because people overestimate the value of what they have and underestimate the value of what they may gain by giving that up."
- James Belasco and Ralph Stayer from "Flight of the Buffalo"[6]

O vercoming internal reluctance to make progress, confront offense or forward the mission, is key to appropriate management of self. At the heart of your own personal resistance is likely some form of self-doubt, probably mixed together with politically correct vacillation. It may sound like this, "Who am I to say this is wrong?" Another favorite is "We all have our faults." Usually self-doubt and anxieties around confronting resistance are rooted in the core relationship we have with our self. It is usually a sign of fear-based living.

Training as a therapist has taught me that people will go to great lengths to "make friends" with their fears. Usually these fears contribute to reluctance to make progress toward your family or organization's goals. These dysfunctional fears often serve an odd but ongoing purpose that keeps you stuck. Despite the chronic suffering these fears inflict, you find some strange reward for maintaining their infliction because they hold off some other pain. As odd as it seems, most people are likely to maintain these chronic patterns for years. They form enough of an obstacle to prevent progress, but not so much that you can't live okay today. It is here people get stuck in either slow death or dispassionate living.

Training as a pastor has taught me this is the nature of sin. It is an internal reflex to slowly "implode." Education as a therapist has trained me to recognize self-defeating behaviors. Training as a leader has taught me it's hard to find mission momentum in the midst of all the resistance to meeting resistance. Especially in a church or community setting, everyone wants to be nice, even if being nice is what's killing you, or destroying the mission.

It is like inhaling a cigarette while thinking "this is killing me." It is foregoing an opportunity to share the joy of your faith or to discipline a teenager for fear of the resistance to either process. It is choosing to avoid loving confrontation, and instead, opting for doing nothing at all except hope it will all magically go away.

It is not a natural tendency to move toward what will do you or others the most good. An appropriate love of self is not as easily befriended as a dysfunction or a fear you've grown accustomed to having around. You may have caught yourself putting up with something just because you didn't want to go through the work of changing it. Love of self and taking care of yourself seems to always slip away into self-defeating patterns in part just because they are easier – for the time being.

Every person on the planet has and will continue to experience resistance to love of self, to love of neighbor, and to the love of the Lord our God. There is a curious reflex in humanity to order self-defeating behaviors through the car window and scarf them down. There is a common destructive pattern to interpret events for their impact on your pleasure and convenience before you consider the long-term benefits of the mission on which you've been sent. Your omission of fruits and vegetables in your diet is not because you don't like bananas or broccoli, but because you can't get them in the vending machine at work.

Going out looking for resistance to conquer is not the call here. This is not about blasting your way through the thick head of your co-worker because he's in your way at the water cooler. The deeper point is the continual deflection of resistance as part of your own dysfunction. Daily trips through convenience stores for a processed lunch sealed in plastic will not prepare you for the hard work of loving and leading. When you ignore the weeds in your yard, you spare yourself a lot of difficult yard work, but it doesn't help make friends in the neighborhood where they have manicured lawns. It is this reluctance to encounter resistance that sets you up for short-term gains and long-term loss.

When you do not love yourself the way God loves you, it's harder to pay the high price real love demands. Real loving costs you – big time! Ask the parent sitting up all night next to a child suffering cancer and its treatments. Ask the wife of fifty-plus years about the cost of loving as she cares for her dying husband. Ask the spouse who chooses to stay in the marriage after a partner's infidelity. Real love costs.

In the same manner it costs you to show real love to yourself in the same way God has loved you. Since your value to Jesus is so high, you're worth moving through the reluctance you feel to speak up for yourself when others speak poorly about you. You're worth the effort to overcome the resistance within to train a four year old how to pick up toys. You're worth the time to walk, or jog in the park, instead of pushing through another report at your desk. You're worth the time and effort it takes to build relationships, to risk being known and getting to know others. When you love yourself the way God loves you, you're willing to pay the price for the things necessary to take care of yourself. When you love yourself the way God loves you, a sense of gratitude surfaces that guides you into appropriate gratification and away from the instant forms of gratification available everywhere. Grateful for what God has done, you steward yourself as God's gift. You want to make certain you take better care of your body, mind and soul. You appreciate how a healthy soul encourages the same health in others.

If I gave you an $80,000.00 luxury car on your 16th birthday, you'd likely be extremely grateful. If I told you it was the last car you'd ever receive, my guess is you would be that much more careful to drive it safely and maintain it really well. Now, suppose you drove the car into a muddy bottom lake after a night of drinking. How might you feel as you walk away from the car submerged with only a corner of the trunk showing? Now imagine I came along and hired a company to retrieve it from the lake and restore it to perfection – all at my expense? Lastly consider how you might respond if I parked it in your driveway and gave it to you once again? You only have one life, one body, one soul and one life to take care of it. Forgiveness is the restorative process. Parking it in your driveway is God's idea of personal attention. But now you still have to drive carefully, do timely maintenance and take care of the gift.

The analogy is intended to give you some inspiration and motivation to love yourself as God has loved you. He created you as precious and valuable. God bought you back at the price of his Son. He places you back on the road of life. If you love yourself as God love you, your typical resistance to resistance will melt away out of gratitude for how valued you really are. You're worth moving through the resistance to resistance because of what God has done for you! The decision to move through your resistance to resistance starts off hard and sometimes gets harder after that. But a rewarding sense of accomplishment and purpose fuels your desire to wake up in the morning and do it again.

What does this mean?

The reluctance you feel to confront your neighbor about his barking dog, for example, is an example of your resistance to meeting resistance. The way you allow "good enough" work to pass, instead of insisting on "great work" is another example of what first must be overcome to encourage others to excel.

Recognizing your resistance to resistance and overcoming it through a balanced focus between the mission and the people on the mission allows you to thrive as a leader.

What can you do?

Anticipate personal reluctance by planning for it. By understanding your own resistance to meeting resistance, you'll be far more likely to stay the course of your mission. By anticipating your own personal resistance, you'll be able to practice and prepare yourself for times of resistance and move toward excellence and mastery. This is accomplished by beginning internally – working first on yourself then on others. Whether it is coaching a little league baseball team or completing a project with a work team, you'll need to prepare to move through your own resistance before loving or leading others through their own resistance.

Chapter 13

Fear is Infectious

ఇమ్మ

*"The strength and power of despotism consists wholly
in the fear of resistance."*
— Thomas Paine

Fear is contagious. Worse yet, fear is infectious.

In fact, researchers claim fear is in large part biologically contagious. Apparently frightened people may be giving off discreet signals from their sweat glands that are picked up by others. People who are afraid give off "pheromones" that may trigger parts of the brain associated with fear. It seems that others close by pick up the scent and, at one level or another, become alarmed as well. Fear is transmitted across powerful non-verbal channels.

I was privileged to lead a mission team from the US to Kenya. The last day before the long journey home, we toured the Trans Mara region, with its tens of thousands of acres of African wildlife. We were led by an experienced guide and given personal attention by the delightful Masai warrior who was also a pastor. We came amazingly close to wildlife. The Masai-Pastor's instructions put our team at ease, as well as provided amazing photo opportunities of hyenas, wildebeests, even up close encounters with lions and lioness.

On one exceptional occasion our Masai Pastor instructed the driver to pull forward along a narrow path. As the driver idled forward the view was incredible. We were perpendicular to a lumbering herd of about twenty elephants. They were only about fifty yards away and moving toward us at a relaxed pace. I felt like I was shrinking in size as they approached and began to slowly circulate around us. I noticed our Masai Pastor enjoying us enjoying the experience. His comfort level gave me great comfort while literally being surrounded by tons of elephants.

Then, his look changed. A large male stopped by a small bush in front of us, as though taking a post. Although the rest of the herd kept lumbering around us, this one bull elephant seemed to stand guard. My primary cause for alarm was the look in the eyes of our Masai protector. It seemed he knew something I did not. The look in his eyes told the story. They changed from delight to concern. I tried to see what he was noticing as he turned quickly to look behind, then in front again. I knew nothing of elephant herd behavior and even less about what to do while in the middle of them. My anxieties rose, not necessarily from being surrounded by elephants, but by the concerned look in the eyes of our Masai Pastor while being surrounded by a herd of elephants.

A minute that felt much longer than that passed. The bull elephant moved on at a slightly quicker pace to get in step with those who had lumbered around us. Our Masai Pastor eyes brightened with his familiar mischievous glint. I relaxed as I watched the backside of elephants lumber off into the distance.

Fear is communicated on multiple channels and in multiple languages – some recognizable, most not. Fear is sensed, and picked up by those around you who are looking for protection in the middle of tons of troubles. Fear is contagious.

This isn't necessarily a bad thing. Your natural ability to communicate fear on multiple levels can alert and protect people around you from dangers. Vigilance in unsafe neighborhoods is a good thing. When danger is real and evident in war zones, fear is both natural and protective. In the Trans Mara of Kenya, a healthy respect for carnivores can keep you from being some-one's dinner.

The problem has more to do with being afraid of things that are good for you, like intimacy, for example. If you're afraid of intimacy, it can interfere with a basic human need you're seeking to fulfill. Others are "warned" when they draw closer, so intimacy itself becomes more difficult to achieve when you're afraid of being known. What is at risk is your personal sense of well being that is derived from being closely connected to another. You com-municate your anxiety in subtle ways to your friend. The fear begins to interfere with your friendship, so you withdraw. This self-defeating pattern can spiral as you become more afraid of what you need increasing fear and decreasing the chance of finding the human connection designed to diminish the fear of intimacy.

One of those human needs relevant to *The Love Paradox* is a Biblical love of self. If you are afraid of a Biblical love of self for fear of seeming, or becoming selfish, for example, you are missing out on God's gift to you. Your fear is communicated and others may be less likely to seek an appropriate stewardship of self, because it seems it might be perceived as indulgent. Many a mom has anxiously avoided respite time from young children out of an overdeveloped sense of duty from her own fear of not being a good mother.

When you perceive love of self as indulgent, oddly enough, you may end up diminishing the potential for service to others. Professional hockey players frequently rotate off the ice for rest. The entire team and the goal to win would both be in danger if one of them refused to rotate off for fear of looking tired. Key basketball players are rested at the end of the third quarter that they might have the energy for peak performance at the end of the game. No matter the score, the need for rest is weighed against what is most important – the score at the end of the game.

Stewardship of self is productive for you and good for the entire team you're leading. Some might say it is even alluring. It looks good on you and invites other people to be at ease around you.

When you are a good steward of self, you are able to discern the difference between taking care of yourself for the sake of others and being afraid to appear weak or indulgent. If you are afraid to seek respite, for fear of "how it looks" to others, your fear is putting larger goals at risk and communicated to those working with you. In marriages, friendships or corporate partnerships, *this is a birthplace of imbalance.* One person continues to over-function while another learns to under-function. One person watches the kids, the other the game on TV. One person carries the burdens of progress while others enjoy its results. The fact this occurs is probably obvious to you. The fact that is often born of being afraid of selfishness may be less visible.

This isn't saying that sacrificial efforts aren't important. They are. However, when you give the gift of sacrifice, it is important it is intentionally given – not done out of fear. If you decide to volunteer to have your salary reduced by 10% so that your organization might receive the benefit and make it through difficult financial times, your gift is your sacrifice. When the gift is unfairly taken from you, and you say nothing to object to it, there is a greater likelihood of resentment along with diminished gifts of service.

You know you're afraid when the appearance of busyness is more important than resting and preparing for busier times. Even if I knew there was a busy season ahead and some down time would prepare me for a busier time, I often neglected the rest I needed for some real or imagined fear of what someone might say. Have you ever tried to look busy even though you needed a break? You knew others would not receive it well. I've been anxious about taking time for me from a fear of looking selfish to others. I allowed others to define my schedule because of my reluctance to find refreshment for the challenges ahead. I recall a time when a coworker spoke of my regular workout routine as a way to escape what I was really "supposed to be doing."

He used the word "spa" instead of health club or gym, and pronounced it in feigned indulgence as if I was going for my daily massage. Such pronouncements illustrate interesting jealousies. The problem is they typically have some impact on appropriate personal management even when you wish they did not.

Do not be afraid of indulging in your pursuit of Biblical love of self! The *fear* of becoming selfish diminishes the potential for your act of service. Fear increases the potential for sulking service as opposed to vibrant servanthood. Do not be afraid of becoming selfish anymore than being afraid to eat for fear of gluttony, or being afraid to love for fear of enjoying it too much.

You're often afraid because personal responsibility is a first cousin of spiritual surrender. It works like this. When you begin an adventure you engage in it without assurance of how it will turn out. That's the reason it's called an adventure! You don't know how the campaign will end. You can't predict what your children will become. You can't forecast the storms that crop up along the journey. So, your fear of what you don't know, or what might happen, is at least a strong temptation to initiate a poor stewardship of self - with which you are much more familiar. This is usually the point at which you say, "I'd like to _____ but I can't because I'm _____.

You'd like to learn to fly, but can't because of you don't have the time. You'd like to start your own business, but can't because you don't want to take the risk. You'd like to compete in a triathlon but don't want to give up chip and dip late at night. You'd like to go back for your GED or your bachelor's or your MBA, but can't because you can't afford it.

Consider how fear of taking responsibility for your well being robs you of experiences of growth and challenge. Because you've had one too many drinks, slept too long or stayed too busy, you've missed contributing to a relationship with a life-shaping experience with another person. By not showing up, you've allowed a vacuum to be formed, perhaps filled, by the quickest fix available.

I invite you to take the risk of responsibility - to show up. More than a nice gesture, this is a sacred calling to be present in order to bless others.

The difficult problem with not showing up is that unrealized dreams are invisible. So, you don't miss what's not there. When something is left undone, it's usually hard to imagine it created and completed. Fear, it seems, and especially fear of responsibility, robs you of what you have, who you are, and also what you could be. Personally I believe losing potential may be the worst loss of all. Personally I believe dreams undreamed are more damaging than nightmares.

Clearly things like self-centeredness, gluttony and other forms of self-centeredness can consume and lead to broken relationships, even death. (Galatians 5.16*f*) It is spiritually sound to develop a healthy respect for - rather than a fear of these things because they become their own prisons. The salvation Jesus provides, and the power granted by the Spirit will supply what is necessary to practice a Biblical stewardship of self. In its simplest terms this is a "fearless" love of self. There's something alluring about someone who is mature enough to stand in the tension. There is something attractive about someone who is able to be adventurous without being foolish.

Consider the enjoyment our team experienced in Africa in the Trans Mara, in part due to the person of Masai Pastor. Beyond his native familiarity with the region, his calm sense of self in the context placed our team at ease. People who are "comfortable in their own skin" call you to move toward them. Their presence allows for you to be present with them. You can have your own opinions, and anticipate others in return without willfulness or difficult debate.

In general, people find it difficult to define exactly what it is about someone who actually illustrates a Biblical love of self. You'll likely hear descriptions and phrases like, "There's just something about her...." You're likely unable to identify exactly why you're trusting of someone you don't know very well. The chances are good they are exercising a well defined sense of self. People will say, "He's confident." Others might describe the attractiveness in physical terms. "I like the way he carries himself."

What happens is that an appropriate Biblical love of self replaces infectious fear with an alluring and inviting presence. The good news is that the way you are valued by Jesus impacts your soul in such a way that people are drawn to your security. The confidence that bubbles up from within is inviting. People enjoy being around such love – even when they don't recognize that is your own Biblical love of self that is at the core.

Yes, fear is infectious, but a Biblical love of self is alluring!

What does this mean?

Managing your fear is key to staying the course and staying connected. Non-verbally, silently, fear is communicated to others and is likely to interfere with staying the course toward your goals. Accepting a Biblical love of self allows you to more easily move toward others in an internal sense of security that allows for more adventure. Faith and fear cannot coexist. Your relationship with God will both increase your faith and thereby diminish your fear.

What can you do?

Begin with your personal relationship to God. It too is contagious. Fear is typically triggered pretty easily, while trust has to be nurtured. So, anticipate set backs, but continue to look to God, even when you're afraid. This will allow you to practice stepping forward when you most feel like stepping backwards. Rather than trying to elicit acceptance from others, you find acceptance from God, which allows you to move toward others freer from expectations. Practice moving toward someone when you're afraid of what they may say next. These mini-adventures gradually open up to larger ones. Keep your eye on the mission and your heart with the people around you.

Chapter 14

"The Unregulated"
Are Like Cancer Cells

~

"Bitterness is like cancer. It eats upon the host."
— Maya Angelou, American Poet

Newton's third law of motion says that for each action there is an equal and opposite reaction.[7] In the spiritual realm, for each blessing your presence brings, there is often an opposing desire to remove it. Although fears usually are birthed within you, there may also be people hoping to make you afraid to progress forward. These fear mongers can often bring their resistance with the power of cancer.

The human body grows through the process of cellular replication. Your cells multiply by dividing in a process called mitosis. You began as an embryo cell that divided into two, then four, then eight cells and so on till you became who you are today. The marvelously complex process provides for cells to "differentiate." That is, each takes up a specific task in your body and communicates to other cells within specific boundaries. Each cell is separate from another, but has permeable boundaries to keep it connected and working together with the cells around it.

On occasion, however, the regulation process goes horribly wrong. The division of cells is unchecked and boundaries are violated. The communication between cells goes poorly. When this happens, these "unregulated" cells cause real trouble. They abandon their healthy function for a destructive one. They cross over designated boundaries to cause harm to other cells. Left unchecked, these unregulated cells have the power to completely destroy the host and itself in the process. This "unregulated" process is the nature of cancer. It's also the nature of carcinogenic people.

In a very similar fashion unregulated people run amok at the expense of the whole organization. They behave like an aggressive cancer. Unregulated people practice a sel*fish* love that violates healthy balanced relationships. These people do not seek what is best for the group or family, but only what is best for themselves. There is a type of cancer called sarcoma that takes its name from the Greek word, "*sarx*" meaning, "*of the flesh*." St. Paul used this word to illustrate a stark contrast between the works of God's Spirit and the works of the selfish. He says,

> *"Those who live according to the sinful nature have their minds set on what that nature desires; but those who live in accordance with the Spirit have their minds set on what the Spirit desires.* (Romans 8.5)

A human sarcoma is a person who thrives by the desires of the sinful nature. They seem to live to intentionally interfere in the lives of others. He/she uses the family, organization or corporation for personal gain. This can be true of a co-worker, a congregational member at a council meeting or an alcoholic in a family.

It does not take much imagination to see the similarity between a practicing alcoholic, raging at the kids and a cancer cell aggressively forcing its way through neighboring cell walls. It's pretty easy to see the cancer-like connection between a coworker who maliciously undermines others at the expense of the work team relationships. These human sarcomas will continue without interruption even as relationships deteriorate and productivity declines. It's not much of a leap to watch someone take over a meeting by deriding leadership with negative comments and then gloat, as the purpose of the meeting is lost to debate. The "unregulated" are like cancer cells. Their influence spreads without concern for others. They cause harm in others and may even destroy the host (small group, work group, company, family) in which they live.

Here's a true story of a human sarcoma. An argument began in a church council meeting between a pastor and a member of the council. After the meeting, the argument spilled out into the parking lot. In the heat of debate with the council member waving his finger, the pastor had a heart attack and died. The accuser showed no remorse, commenting that the pastor was overweight anyway.[8] This is the cancer-like behavior of the "unregulated." Like the deadly course of sarcoma, it begins with smaller chronic issues that develop into much larger "tumors" that eventually harm the spirit – if not kill the person.

These unregulated behaviors pop up like cancerous tumors and can be found in places like a pending divorce or custody battle when one or the other partner becomes determined to harm the other. Spiritual markers for these cancerous tumors could be a DUI, the receipt from a credit card shopping binge, or loud careless words directed at the kids. Any of these can serve as the indicator of underlying spiritual immaturity that behaves like a cancer eating away at healthy spiritual tissue. In each of these examples an individual's behavior is at the expense of the group or family. In each case they cannot or will not stop on their own. Their cancerous behavior looks like passion, but is actually immaturity out of control – unable and unwilling to control itself.

This is not God's design. These spiritual and emotional cancer cells are an obstacle to healthy life and relationships. These people will not stop with reasonable conversation, pleading or negotiations. In my leadership experience, my hesitation to curb these behaviors was more costly than the price to put aside current mission goals and confront these people head on. I have learned that your response to these spiritual and emotional cancers needs to be as aggressive as the cancer itself. It is critical to address cancerous people early on and not allow yourself to be caught off guard by their fervor. You are not called on to be the recipient of bullying, abuse, or rage. This never defines Christian faithfulness. Jesus' call to "turn the other cheek" (Matthew 5.39) is a call to love the wicked – not an open invitation for the cruel to have their way. It's an invitation to intentionally love instead of reacting out of resentment or other dark passions.

There is nothing spiritually noble about allowing carcinogenic people to ruin you or the organization you serve. I have ministered to abused wives who had to be convinced their toleration of abuse was not love of God, themselves or even the abuser. In most of these cases people had to be coached and encouraged to what I have nicknamed "sacred self-regulation."

The Bible defines this sacred self-regulation as a "theology of the cross." Through Jesus' sufferings God has bought us back and called us to be his. You practice this "theology of the cross" through the intentional decisions to forego short cuts, quick fixes or reactive aggression. (1 Corinthians 1:18-25) Exercising a theology of the cross means not allowing the unregulated to run and ruin with abandon. Instead it means to decide ahead of time to respond lovingly, powerfully and intentionally in all circumstances so that God is glorified and the mission is forwarded.

Living day to day by a theology of the cross may mean that you forego a promotion because you refuse to take a position that is likely to provide your family with more money, but less of you. It may mean offering forgiveness to those who ask even when you'd prefer to get even. In these instances and so many others, lifestyle decisions are made based on God's larger mission and your intention to further that mission – even at cost to your own convenience.

However, a theology of the cross lifestyle doesn't overtake you and wear you down like lymphoma. By the power of God's

Spirit, you intentionally do the right thing and trust God through the process. Living a theology of the cross is more like accepting the mission no matter the cost. As a result of God's process, you are stronger when it seems you are weaker. As a result of God's Spirit working within you, you are content to know insults, hardships, persecutions, calamities and other ungodly forms of spiritual immaturity not as some spiritual form of self-abuse, but because they highlight the strong sense of purpose God has placed inside you. (2 Corinthians 12.10)

Sacred self-regulation – especially in the company of those who are "unregulated" comes from God's gift of a new way of thinking and seeing your self. In God's paradoxical way, it's the death to selfishness that raises a new self to be valued and well managed. It's this new highly valuable self that is full of mission and purpose. It's this Spirit empowered, self-regulated person that will sacrifice for the sake of the mission, but not for the sake of convenience or someone else's bullying.

An adult child of an alcoholic is practicing a sacred self-regulation when she no longer allows her drunken mom to call her and spew accusations. She stops mistaking her own passivity for loving behavior or Christian teachings and sees the avoidance of confrontation as a tempting shortcut to avoid the discomfort of difficult self-regulation. Instead, when her mom calls, drunk and full of anger, she hangs up and writes an email the next day indicating she will no longer allow herself to be spewed upon.

There are some that believe the deadly parking lot interaction with the pastor who lost his life to conflict was a type of self-sacrifice or modern-day martyrdom. I believe it is more likely the deadly interaction of two unregulated people ending a life prematurely. There's nothing sacred about letting a bully rage on while allowing you and the organization to suffer the consequences for it. Sacred self-regulation could have been illustrated by walking away, or with enough presence of mind, turning toward the unregulated cancer cell and thanking him for his opinion.

In many and varied ways the "unregulated" kill. Just like the fight against cancer, a healthy and robust response is necessary to counter the effect of the "unregulated" on you and the organization to which you belong. This response is best characterized as a lifestyle called a "theology of the cross." Essentially it is a life of sacred self-regulation in difficult circumstances because of the price Jesus paid to redeem you. It means standing up early and firmly against those who are unregulated and then facing the difficult circumstances even when they make you feel uncomfortable. You can trust that God who ordained it will bless doing the right thing.

It means the suffering you go through in life comes from doing the right thing – not from doing nothing while human sarcomas run amok.

What does this mean?

Those who will not be calmed, or those whose fears will not be alleviated, are "unregulated." They act cancer cells that multiply uncontrollably. They lack the desire or will to make adjustments necessary to live well in community. As a result they may end up consuming and destroying the community, in the same way cancer cells end up consuming and destroying the body that hosts it. A "theology of the cross" is dedicated living to the mission, not allowing carcinogenic people to run amok.

What can you do?

Intervene early to curb the unregulated by drawing clear non-negotiable boundaries. Your commitment to do the right thing is absolutely necessary to begin curbing those who will not limit themselves. The earlier the intervention, the better. Churches have church discipline, even seldom utilized excommunication. Organizations have policies that allow them to immediately fire people. Parents have to learn how to apply tough love with immediate consequences. Teams bench players. Associations levy fines. Act early. Act decisively. Don't wait. Don't delay.

Chapter 15

Boundaries As Blessing

"Boundaries are to protect life, not to limit pleasures."
—Ed Cole, Founder of Christian Men's Network

A woman won't stop talking over lunch. She is also abusing pain medications. A man refuses to take 'no' for 'no' on a date. He always shows up late for dates and dinner invitations. A young couple allows their toddler to stay up way too late. They also eat out way too much for their budget. A sincere and hardworking man gets low productivity evaluations because he can't stay focused on the task in front of him. He also doesn't get enough sleep.

What is the common denominator? Each has boundary problems. Each person's boundary problems show up in different areas of their life. Each also sees boundaries as a problem rather than a blessing.

Boundaries are absolutely essential for human existence. They define relationships, community and creation itself. Basically the Bible's creation account is all about boundary setting. Chaos is given definition till it becomes order. Darkness gives way to the clear definition of light. Waters and dry land each find where they end and the other begin. (Job 38)

From the beginning boundaries are illustrations of love not punishment. Loving parents are in a perpetual state of boundary setting because it adds consistency and predictability to family interactions. These boundaries provide for a sense of security. By setting bed times, places you can and can't play, vegetables to cookies ratios and the like, boundaries serve the family, and bless the child. As children and parents grow together they will set more and more relationship boundaries that will help everyone learn what to expect from everyone else and add consistency and predictability to their relationship.

Although the nature, benefits and health of boundaries is a book all its own, the purpose here is to encourage you to develop vision to see their effect in everyday life. Seeing the effect of boundaries and boundary violations in the world gives you eyesight that provides insight into what makes relationships healthy or what keeps them from becoming healthy.

Violations of basic boundaries range from annoying chatter to the injury of violent crimes and rape. Although the crimes against persons is far more painful, both incessant talking and violence means someone is disrespectful, even damaging of another's personal being. Clearly you'll want to flee the violent, and with eyesight that provides insight you'll also be able to avoid or confront those who disrespect others' boundaries in large or small ways.

I know of someone that was known for violating personal and emotional boundaries. He went so far as to invite himself over to friends' homes then spent his time attempting to convince others someone he disliked was mentally ill. Under the guise of caring, he disparaged those who disagreed with him. This doesn't mean that every time someone sticks their nose in your business they are this toxic. But it is meant to illustrate the fundamental link that joins the two. When people disrespect boundaries in one area of life, they are very likely to do so in other areas. When people do not respect boundaries they do what is right in their own eyes.

A friend of mine told of a school board meeting he attended in the St. Louis area that became derailed when someone in a full rage stood up and lunged toward those engaged in debate. Rising and pointing a waving finger, the physically imposing man freighted people in the room. A few minutes later the temper turned on my friend as he was backed against a wall in a threatening fashion. Oddly enough, to the amazement of all present, within a few minutes the tempest-filled man was welcomed back into the meeting – without repercussion from his eruption.

My friend was aghast at leadership's implicit permission giving. Not only was he shocked at their lack of immediate response; he was even more flabbergasted when some minimized the raging behavior. Were people afraid? Was the chair of the meeting going to allow the incident to pass without so much as the request for an apology? When my friend challenged their position, their displeasure turned on him for "elevating it" after it was over.

He said it reminded him of the cycle of abuse in families. In these clearly dysfunctional families, the one who speaks out or seeks help is treated as the identified problem. Enraged people are no respecter of boundaries whether they are abusive husbands or angry board members. In another example illustrating how boundary violations in one area are likely to appear in other areas, my friend discovered the raging man had been fired from his previous job for inappropriate outbursts.

The generalities of this story were shared with my daughter-in-law who is the Director of an inner city after school program in Chicago. She asked my friend if he called the police. He shook his head no. He did not. Since physical violence was potentially present, was the raging man told to leave or escorted out of the building to assure the safety and security of everyone present? He shook his head "no" again. She asked if he was aware both of those things were practiced in the inner city – as a matter of course. He shrugged, "I can see why they would be."

The discussion turned to questions about why this was the case. Why is it that definitive physical and emotional boundaries were well established in inner city Chicago, and totally absent in suburban St. Louis? I think it illustrates a few interesting principles about the unregulated and their disregard for boundaries of people around them.

First, the lack of regulation of boundaries was present as the chairman failed to draw a line between debate and personal attacks. Without the presence of a strong leader ready and capable of taking a stand, implicit permission is granted to push past boundaries courtesy and control. This is as true whether it is a weak father figure who does not invest emotionally in the home or a supervisor that refuses to discipline unsafe behavior on the job. We all know of snotty kids who come from homes where there is little in the way of discipline. Sometimes these misbehaving children are not given life-enhancing boundaries simply because lazy parents see them as too much work. Parents of teens sometimes refuse to provide boundaries out of fear of how the teenager might respond. In all of the cases above, lack of life-giving boundaries leads to degeneration of important relationships.

If leaders, dads, moms, babysitters, substitute teachers, vice-presidents or hockey coaches cannot take a stand, i.e., establish boundaries with loving authority, then those around them will have less "regulation." They will have less of the control necessary to live cooperatively with others. It takes strength of character, time and effort to establish bounds, delineate them and alert those who wander outside them. The depth of such character and effort comes from an appropriate *Biblical love of self* that is itself secured in God's loving boundaries. First you experience them, next re-create them, and lastly coach others how to remain within them.

It flows down like this. God established boundaries throughout creation. He placed you within them that you may flourish. You are called to establish those same boundaries in relationships that they may flourish. You can do this because you have been blessed by the same boundaries you're trying to establish with others.

In times of debate, the leader is called on to draw lines that assure an issue-oriented focus. It's not as though passionate speeches and debates are not allowed. It's not as though objections and negotiations are ignored or censured. It's not as though your teen cannot share a different perspective. They are welcomed – especially in the context of a safe and appropriately controlled environment where people are trying to work cooperatively.

Organizations face complex issues that often require complicated solutions. Families live in constantly changing conditions as children and parents mature. Debate is welcome. I'm thinking about a former Executive Pastor with whom I worked. Because he was responsible for the day-to-day operations we sometimes debated on and off for days to make certain plans were well coordinated and executed. Our partnership and friendship grew as a result of it. When focused on the issues debate clarifies and connects. Debate that crosses the line and degenerates into personal attacks has the opposite effect of debilitating or destroying relationships.

The second lack of regulation in the meeting example came in the obvious rage and outburst. It's the rough equivalent of the two-year old flailing on the kitchen floor. There is little that a leader can do to stop these from occurring – especially if limits were not established early on in the process. There was "unregulated" behavior, and "unregulated" response. Whether it is a toddler pounding on the floor, or someone name calling at a school board hearing, an immediate time out is critical to draw a boundary for those who attempt to live life without them.

A basketball referee's training involves keeping control of the game. There is an art to letting the players play passionately, i.e., push for position or give a hard foul to prevent an easy lay-up. There is just as fine an art to not losing control of the game amidst all the passion and pushing. This is what the technical foul is for. It is the first notice that emotionality rather than basketball is being played out on the floor. I've only seen it once, but after the technical fouls are used up, or control the game no longer, the whistle blows, the refs throw up their hands and call "game over." This is not only intended to prevent physical harm as the possible consequence of passionate playing, but is also recognition that basketball has hit the showers and emotionality is all that's left of the game. It's not basketball being played anymore – it's something else being played out. Therapists have a (grammatically incorrect) turn of the phrase to describe this. *"The issue ain't the issue no more."*

The second lack of unregulated response came when the meeting chair didn't blow his whistle and announce – game over. After such an outburst the meeting isn't a meeting anymore – it's an emotional containment field. From that point on people have been frightened and are now unable to think clearly. Others are angry and repressing their desires to keep the whole meeting from turning into a hockey game. Most are now so conscious of the high emotionality there is little being done with reasonable thinking. Everyone is clearing their heads while finances are on the agenda. School business has hit the showers and emotionality is all that's left of the meeting.

Trying to run a school board or business meeting after someone has raged is like nearly missing a deer on a dark country highway late at night and then trying to do Soduku puzzles. At least for a few moments, you're lucky to remember your phone number, much less figure out the sum of digits necessary to solve the puzzle. Complex problem solving during times of high anxiety is either very difficult or nearly impossible. When your brain has gone into survival mode and flooded everything with adrenaline, calm complex problem solving is unlikely. The leader has to draw boundaries so that everyone can go from an anxious mode to one of reasonable calm.

The final opportunity to draw healthy boundaries during times of high anxiety is what my daughter-in-law pointed out. On the one hand, some external form of consequence should have been imposed. This is particularly true in episodes of rage and personal attacks. On the other hand, the opportunity opens wide the door for forgiveness to walk in the room and reconnect relationships that might have been brutally severed.

The Latin phrase, *ad hominine*, means "against the person." It conveys the difference between debate that is issue focused and a personal attack. If I have issue with your leadership of the work group and I have the maturity to be issue focused, then I might say, "I don't care for the manner in which you delegate tasks without fully explaining your final objective." An *ad hominine* attack is effectively saying to the work group leader, "You suck." It is an attempt to discredit the decisions of the work group leader by personally attacking him in an attempt to persuade (yourself or) others you think he's wrong. The person above inviting himself into the homes of friends was utilizing an *ad hominine* attack by personally targeting character and credibility (instead of addressing decisions or directions in leadership). Sometimes called "demonizing" this behavior also implicitly elevates the accuser to a position of rescuer. Ironically in this way the boundary-violator attempts to look like a savior.

A psychologist I once heard told a story of an angry mom who shouted back to an emotionally distraught elementary child, "I hate you too." Years later, many years later, the young adult could still feel the wound of that *ad hominine* response from his mom. Adults, leaders, those who steward authority are given the responsibility to debate the issue and not attack the character. *Ad hominine* attacks are essentially boundary violations of those unable or unwilling to first manage themselves well.

The boundary-crossing unregulated person acting out in personal attacks harms not only the individual under attack, but also the soul of the organization or family. Personal attacks are hard to witness – even when they are not directed at you individually. They can unsettle the psyche and harm the spirit of everyone involved by striking at a deep emotionally damaging chord. It's like filling the room with a toxic gas of angry emotionality. The toxic air disrupts breathing. People have a natural revulsion – in part for personal protection. An *ad hominine* incident sometimes takes on parable-like power as people tell and retell the story in coffee shops and parking lots – sometimes as a means to process the disturbing emotions.

Yet the opportunity for gospel-centered healing is never more available. The depth of injury such personal attacks produce provides a clear opportunity to glorify God for the gift that reconnects what had been severed. In fact, the greater the injury the more clearly the gospel is a blessing. The process of a bone fracture healing provides a good picture for the mending and strengthening of the soul that occurs through forgiveness. Over time the brokenness is mended through a process that brings strength to the fracture. Over time the use of the previously broken bone is once again restored. In the same way, relationships are restored and strengthened to glorify God.

I am certified as a Critical Incident Stress Management (CISM) counselor. This means I have been trained to minister to those who have observed or rescued others from tragic circumstances. Although the death of children may be the most traumatic, a very close second is discovering people who have suffered abuse at the hands of others. Finding those who are traumatized to the point of being discolored from beatings, takes a huge emotional toll on everyone trying to help out. From police who first arrive on the scene to the emergency room medical personnel, there is suffering from simply being around those who are suffering.

I recently spoke to a Minneapolis newspaper truck driver who delivers papers all night to the vendors who sell them the next day. Near downtown, on a cold night he discovered a small child wandering around wearing only a diaper. Wrapping the child in his coat, after calling 911, he went door-to-door in the middle of the night hoping to find the toddler's home. The incident still clearly had emotional impact years later as he recounted the story. Just being around suffering – especially the suffering of children, injures the soul, sometimes leaving scars for a long time.

Certainly witnessing a personal attack of someone in a school board meeting is far down on the continuum of what might injure your soul. It doesn't compare to what is seen in a month by the city of Detroit's ambulance and rescue personnel. CISM training, and decades in ministry, tells me it still does, however, make it hard for everyone to be engaged with the offensive person. Such deliberate aggression impacts not only the person being attacked, but all those who witness it. This is the case, because in large part, to witness it is to participate in it to some degree. When this happens the organization itself becomes associated with those who personally attack others and allow it to continue. People will inherently avoid organizations; families and friends who allow such damaging, toxic fume filling behavior to go without consequence.

The implicit question seems to be, "Who's next?" or "What happens if he steps over the line to physical violence next time?" Because people are in a self-protective mode, sometimes called a fight or flight posture, they are unable to think clearly and effectively pursue the mission of the organization which requires more complex thinking. All of this results from the lack of defining appropriate boundaries.

This is yet another reason why stewardship of self is so necessary in general, but critical during times of anxious, unregulated behavior when people are running all over personal boundaries. These examples are intended to help you see how even the most minor boundary violations like the chatter from an overly talkative person, can illustrate deeper boundary issues, disorders or even addictions. Yet the best news of this chapter is the realization of how God's power of forgiveness reestablishes relationships and appropriate relationship boundaries. This is an example of the "regulatory" nature of the gospel and its potential to heal through loving forgiveness and the practice of establishing clear boundaries.

What does this mean?

When "the unregulated" run amok like cancer cells, defining boundaries is absolutely essential. It is important to be far enough from toxic people to avoid injury and close enough to provide opportunity for potential connection. Defining boundaries, however, is not enough. Enforcing boundaries defined is important to regulate those who will not regulate themselves. When there is receptivity, the love of God can reestablish appropriate boundaries and their life-giving nature through forgiveness.

What can you do?

Clearly define and enthusiastically enforce healthy boundaries. This should be done as soon as possible. Since the nature of the unregulated is to infringe upon or overpower boundaries, the setting of boundaries should have high fences and be electrically charged. Without the internal controls to live within boundaries, external controls will need to be in place or the mission will suffer, if not be lost altogether as the family or organization fills with emotionally and spiritually toxic fumes.

Chapter 16

Managing Yourself Well
When Others Are In Crisis

ℭℌℨ

*"All seasons are important, but no more so than
the strong season when emotions run high."*
—*Peter Steinke*

A friend who works as a supervisor for a company experiencing lay-offs relayed a story of workers filing multiple grievances against him. He was their foreman on the shop floor and they objected to his enforcement of company policy. Their behavior became more and more abrasive till it included destruction of company property. The foreman was saddened by the mindless escalation in behaviors of the workers that would now end in their dismissal. He was further distressed because he now had to participate in a process that brought them to the end they seemed to be self-destructively seeking. He was aware each of them had families to support. Anyone who has originated a disciplinary action knows the sense of reluctance that often accompanies the process, even when it is the right thing to do.

As noted in the previous chapter, the need for a healthy stewardship of self is critical when the immature ignore healthy boundaries to cause you harm. This chapter focuses on the care for yourself when people around you are suffering. It could be the chronic tension that results from company-wide lay-offs, for example. Sometimes, institutional policy creates its own anxious times. Consider, for example what may happen with implementation of the U.S. Department of Labor's WARN Act.

The Worker Adjustment and Retraining Notification Act (WARN) offers protection to workers, their families and communities by requiring employers to provide sixty days notice in advance of certain plant closings and mass layoffs. Allowing time for families and communities to prepare for upcoming financial stressors gives birth to at least two processes. The first is preparation for the many family adjustments to be made. This time of financial hardship includes difficult or unwelcome shifts in family patterns. Dealing with application for unemployment, searches for new employment, retraining or switching breadwinners in a household are all stress producing. Such interruptions in life interfere with personal plans, hopes and dreams. Compound this with the heightened emotionality in the workplace stress and you have a recipe for disaster.

Emotional numbness at notification of such widespread lay-offs can sprout into anger followed by depression, anger turned inward. With anger and depression clarity and hopefulness are depleted. These powerful emotions show up for work each day under the management of supervisors. If stewardship of self is important on normal workdays, it is critical now. The responsibility of the supervisor is to anticipate anxiety in response to the powerful emotions walking in the door. By first managing self well, a supervisor will recognize the stages of loss that belong to him or her, as well.

Managing yourself will mean finding whatever renewal patterns are necessary to maintain a spirit of connection while everyone is separating. Whether it is improving your bowling game, fixing old cars, or training for a triathlon, physical and emotional refreshment is extremely important. First managing yourself well may mean reading up on company policy, likely to be challenged. Preparing yourself by reading up on the nature of grief being experienced in multiple facets will enable you to anticipate and make plans to ease the climate of your workplace.

First managing yourself well might involve praying for the company and the people you individually know are affected. In this way, even if you may be forbidden from such spiritual conversation at work, your personal consideration of their transition will be communicated in any caring connections you might have opportunity to show. Praying for someone by name brings him or her to mind. This connection, even without their awareness, is communicated subtly, but powerfully.

In this example the introduction of the WARN Act is God's invitation to begin with an assurance of his presence. If you're in the midst of emotional times, or you're the person responsible to lead others through their own painful transitions, reassurance of God's presence provides the stability necessary to walk into an unstable environment. Personal worship practices, even a few minutes of meditation on God's promises, can be wonderful spiritual tools to help you find a place to be grounded in those promises when you need them most.

It's your calling and God's invitation to take a look at all aspects of your life in response to the increased emotional toll necessary to assist others. This is particularly important when working with large numbers of people going through transition together. For example, you may have been knocking out your MBA in the evenings in addition to playing in two softball leagues. First managing yourself well is the invitation to revisit your investment in relationships before advanced degree work. Perhaps you drop one MBA class and a softball league in exchange for a designated date night. Since a higher percentage of people will be looking at you with suspect eyes at work, seeing the face of friends can feed your spirit.

Remember, *things change when you show up*. There are dozens of subtle cues that communicate your hopeful attitude and openness to what people are experiencing. Your hopeful presence translates into physical signs such as posture, eye contact, the nature of your smile and voice tone. Even if you can't comprehend the many physical, emotional and spiritual cues of your presence, (and you can't), revel in the reality that God created everything to be interconnected. This means the investment you've made at home in your private life is impacting people and productivity at work. It means you'll be able to better connect with people to encourage them to work cooperatively, even if it's only for a short while longer.

You and I both know people who will be destructive no matter how hopeful or loving you may be. The self-regulation helpful in these circumstances is to accept the role of one who will have the integrity to allow the consequences of people's destructive choices. This is what produced the greatest sadness in my foreman friend. I recognized it because I have coached parents through this same sadness when adolescent behavior became self-destructive. I have walked with spouses who have witnessed their partner destroy their marriage, and in the end, themselves.

The invitation of God is *to stay the course and stay connected.* Staying the course for my foreman friend meant continuously upping the disciplinary ante till the next level administration, security and the police were called in for formal investigation. Staying connected meant continuing dialogue with polite but firm warnings, even as the behavior escalated. Doing both at the same time – precisely when there is the temptation to avoid the difficult tension is good for the company. But, better yet, it is good for the spiritual and emotional growth of those in leadership.

Staying connected with dissenters and troublemakers is often a difficult and distasteful task. This is true, in part, because of the emotional toll it takes to hold to such a sensitive balance. I once sat down with a father whose tears described his suffering at his son's escalating drug related behaviors. In order to shield his younger children from his son's unregulated behavior, he had to tell his son that he was no longer welcome in their home as long as these out of control behaviors persisted. The decision, reached over many months and in conjunction with his wife, had to be done to protect younger children, but it was still devastating. The dad's heart was breaking.

In another incident I was called to a hospital emergency room in the middle of the night where a young, manic-depressive young man was being tended to by a trauma team. In the middle of the night, at home, he attempted to take his life by hanging himself. But he did not die. Although his brain was swelling from the trauma, and would eventually take his life, over the next eleven hours, heroic life-saving efforts were underway at this predawn moment.

I stood by his mom and her friend, praying, embracing, and crying while we witnessed her son's heaving from another heart attack. The trauma team worked amazingly quickly with expert integration. The head medical person paced at the foot of the bed, hands behind her back listening as each person blurted out medical measurements and treatments. It sounded like people talking fast in a foreign language. With intensity and calm, she issued orders, asked questions and assessed progress. It was amazing and frightening to observe.

When diagnostics informed us medical science could do nothing but make him comfortable for death, grief swelled to overwhelming proportions. As more and more family and friends arrived, shared grief and trauma poured out in embraces. His dad was out of town on business, but kept in contact as he traveled home. We all prayed for his quick, safe arrival to say goodbye to his son. Upon his arrival, only minutes before the medical personnel prepped for harvesting organs, all of us witnessed the dad's bitter tears as he embraced the reality of the past eleven hours of shock, trauma, hope, lost hope and helpless grief.

Throughout this time, I had to be present enough to minister to some of life's deepest pain, and separate enough to be effective in it. It was exhausting. On only a few hours sleep, I was ministering to a mom at the worst moment of her life. As dawn and a few friends arrived I would take momentary breaks by taking some deep breaths outside, stretching to release the tension building up, and praying – constantly praying. When a group of about fifteen people had surrounded the mom and the news of the young man's pending death was now certain, I stepped away to a waiting room for a moment. Everyone was told it would be a while before the young man could be seen again. I used the time to call Marilouise. Her voice alone served to provide some needed peace. After I hung up I put my chair against a wall and tilted my head back for a ten-minute catnap. I awoke ready for what would soon be a time of final good-byes and very deep and very painful grief.

Even during times of extreme anxiety, you as caregiver are called on to find ways to care for yourself in order to be most fully present for those in crisis. Whether it is the slow disintegration of a co-worker or the sudden suicide of a friend, caring for your self is essential to best minister to those experiencing very difficult times. They need more of you than ever.

What does this mean?

Managing yourself well while others are in crisis calls for a formidable stewardship of self especially if you have to witness self-destruction while not participating in it or becoming reactive to it. This is why it is so critical to *The Love Paradox* to experience the love God has for you and then be a good steward of the self God has so valued. It's done for the sake of those who are walking beside people in trying times to absorb the powerful emotions that can be a part of your gift of presence. Staying separate but connected to people is usually not easy, but never harder than through times of other's crisis.

What should I do?

First, decide ahead of time to stand beside those who are self-destructing. You want to be close enough to love and lead but far enough away to avoid being hurt by them. Secondly, since it is emotionally draining to be around others in crisis, you are called on to take whatever steps, however small, to enhance your ability to be fully present to those in deep distress. Thirdly, resist getting sucked into the emotional vortex around those in crisis. You cannot help by experiencing their anxiety with them. You can help most by standing steadfastly beside them.

Chapter 17

Death by a Thousand Cuts

"You can die the death of a thousand cuts very easily."
- Adam Cummings

The pastor who died in the parking lot argument undoubtedly made the news. It qualified as newsworthy because of the trauma and unusual nature of the event. Pastors don't normally die in parking lots.

On the other hand, come to think of it, pastors may indeed die in parking lots – cumulative "parking lot incidents" over the years of people talking *about* rather than *to* one another. Actually, I think a great deal of anyone's emotional drain comes from others talking about rather than to others. Office politics, back door deals happen everywhere institutions are formed. However, the fact that these immaturities commonly occur everywhere doesn't diminish the negative impact it has on leaders. Just because you get used to something doesn't mean it's good for you. In fact, the chronic stress suffered by leaders can be much more damaging than the blows of acute stress. At least with acute stress, you're very aware you have to muster your defenses. You have to decide whether to stay and fight or run away and hide.

However, in the slow penetrating progress of chronic stress, the "fight or flight" alarm is not sounded. There's not enough pressure or threat at any one time to trigger the brain's warning mechanisms. As a result, as you go about your daily business, you ever so slowly become disconnected from yourself, people you love and the people you serve. As a result of this day-in day-out-emotional erosion, the mission you're working will end up harming you, or even silently killing you. Experiencing the slow build up of chronic stress is like very gradually increasing the carbon monoxide levels in your home over a three-year period. Eventually a fatal level of carbon monoxide will kill you, but it's hard to say what night that will happen.

You are created and designed to handle intermittent acute stress. In fact, your spirit, mind and body often respond to acute stress with renewed strength. Acute stress can be as helpful as breaking down muscle tissue during weight training. It's what will build a stronger muscle. The cliché "If it doesn't kill you, it will make you stronger" describes the potential benefit to working through acute stress.

On the other hand, slowly escalating chronic stress gradually and invisibly overwhelms, day in day out, week in week out, year in year out. As the slow accumulation of the carbon monoxide of chronic stress slowly rises, people tend to develop progressively worse and worse symptoms. These tend to move from distracting behaviors like too much TV to at-risk behaviors such as too much eating. Eating as an escape provides momentary pleasurable satisfaction when life seems to lack moments of satisfaction. By itself, this isn't so bad because food, dining and a little wine with it all is designed to produce a pleasurable effect. The difference, however, lies in the spiritual and emotional reasons for eating and drinking.

To eat or drink as a means to gain a full sense of satisfaction can be a good thing. To eat or drink as an attempt to fill the underlying sense of depletion eating away at you simply won't work. It's like trying to exercise more as the carbon monoxide level continues to rise. The problem exercise is trying to fix isn't what's killing you. If the spiritual emotional depletion is not dealt with directly, food, drink or almost anything providing momentary pleasure fills in the satisfaction gap, but that's not what's killing you. The problem is not that this pleasure fix doesn't work – but that it doesn't work *for long*. When the satisfaction of food wears away and the underlying dissatisfaction returns, chances are more and more food or drink will be necessary to fill the gap from the temporary pleasure fix you're using. This chronic downward spiraling looks like this.

The company you work for, the organization you serve, or the family to which you belong, do not need you less because you have less to give as your chronic depletion drags on. Your presence and the gift of relationship it provides is no less important than before even though your spiritual and emotional resources have slowly diminished. A spiraling, slow swirling vortex begins to form in your soul. It starts gradually but then swirls more quickly as your need for full-fill-ment grows. People around you may sense your withdrawal. More requests for your interaction come from those you are called to love and lead. The problem is you have less spiritual and emotional resources available to participate. This frustration to be more engaged further depletes already diminishing spiritual and emotional energy. This is turn creates a larger vacuum experienced by those around you. The ensnaring effect has power because it is so slowly experienced and so invisibly causes problems. It's not uncommon for people to attribute their growing lethargy to some physical cause. You might say, "I just need more sleep" when the reality is your sleep is interrupted because you need more fulfillment in your life and relationships.

This slow decline toward depletion is often identified as burnout or chronic low-level depression. This slow decline toward depletion is typically engaged outside your own awareness. This is when first managing yourself well is especially difficult. It is when the downward spiraling process is not registering on your conscious radar. In other words, the damaging dynamics of the spiritually and emotionally immature continue to undermine your well-being, but you don't have a clue it's happening to you. These are some of the most toxic scenarios in families or organizations.

Usually, the cruel do not have the patience to exercise slow aggression. Cruel people typically want destruction quickly and visibly. On occasion, however, there are those who actually desire to wear you down slowly. These are the people that do more than experience spiritual/emotional anxiety. They have become their suffering. These are people who have typically experienced great family sorrow, injustice or dysfunction. I learned from a mentor, Pete Steinke, they are not anxious as much as they are their anxiety. They're the ones volunteering for positions that may carry little nuggets of authority, stepping forward for volunteer coaching in the community or desperately seeking to be head of the neighborhood association or leaders on school committees. The worst of these produce terrible headlines as their control of others reaches criminal proportions.

This is the slow spiraling pattern that defines "death by a thousand cuts." This is an ancient Chinese torture that slowly cut victims with enough injury to bleed, but with the intention to prolong life in order to prolong the pain. Progressively more of the body would be injured for physically excruciating punishment. Granted this actual practice, outlawed in China since 1905, is only a metaphor for the slow invisible spiraling of chronic stress. It is, however, a metaphor that works.

I have counseled families and children of these types of parents who have seen their child as an interruption in their happiness pursuit. Although abortion might be considered the ultimate act of aggression toward the unwanted, this is more like an abortion of the soul in slow motion. Sometimes these children move into adulthood with little inherent ability to connect to others and to develop relationships necessary for healing. Having spent childhood and adolescence trying to survive one more cut, their natural survival technique, distancing and defensiveness interferes with their desire or ability to connect with others. Essentially, that which helped them survive is what now holds them captive.

Without knowing it, the child grows up suffering from the harmful habits of immature parents. These parents often have a dysfunctional need to have the child around in order to have a readily available victim to blame for life's disappointments. This child is sometimes called, the "identified patient." In the best of families, dysfunction tends to move around. In the healthiest families, everyone takes turns having a problem. You've heard it from parents who say something like, "I just got Billy over his math anxiety and now Jane wants to quit dance because her friend quit. It's always something."

In the unhealthiest families, in the most dysfunctional organizations, "the problem" becomes fixed on one person. I had a grown man recall his upbringing by an alcoholic father. In his words, "If something went wrong in the neighborhood, I got the crap beat out of me." In congregations when there is a short tenure and a quick sequence of lead pastors, there is a high probability the senior pastor has become the identified patient. In a sense, the dysfunction speaks, "Any problems in the neighborhood are because of this guy. Let's clean up the neighborhood by blaming him."

The typical undermining behavior of those who practice this torture is targeted at an individual, usually a leader within the organization, as a means of punishment for some perceived violation. Always blaming problems on the leader is like trying to cure a cold by treating a runny nose. You can tell when your nose dries up, but it only means the underlying virus is less visible.

In these "identified patient" families or organizations, there is usually some degree of conscious choice to the harm being caused. Granted, all of us harm others, sometimes intentionally. However in this "death by a thousand cuts" there is a consistency over time targeted at an "identified patient" that wreaks spiritual devastation. Like the child in a dysfunctional family, the leaders of an organization with this problem often do not know they are being undercut. It typically requires that a child grows up before she/he finds enough distance from the damaging parents that allows for the realization of what was going on to be possible. In a similar way, it's only after targeted leadership has found some level of space and objectivity that the camouflaged behavior of the toxic people can be addressed.

The problem is that the depletion of energy is tiring and can keep the repetitive nature of the cycle intact for years. It may go something like this. A leader enters the system and by his/her sheer presence begins to shift relationships. Things look and feel different just because the interactions of friendships and conversations are all different. This doesn't have anything to do with strategic direction, visioning or planning. A shift begins because relationships aren't something, they're everything. Independent of views and perspectives, the relationships are different. This difference is experienced by the immature as a problem in large part because it violates expectations. Each new relationship is experienced with grief/anger because things aren't the way they were before. These people resist these new relationships by raising small but significant objections to seemingly insignificant matters. These are the potential stirrings of what can become death by a thousand cuts.

This is true because the leader is likely unaware of these small and subtle, but numerous and persistent cuts to him/her personally. This secret resistance is intentionally designed to continue because it is fueled by new growth and new relationships. As a result there is a depletion of energy and resiliency that invisibly worsens over time. It is initiated from the complaints of those stuck with an "identified patient" mentality. Little by little, it takes more and more time to accomplish everyday tasks because little cuts aren't given time to heal before new, small cuts are inflicted. The energy necessary for significant change of direction or new creative possibilities is increasingly difficult because there is little opportunity for replenishment when the goal of the immature is to find one more small way to cut into the progress of leadership.

In effect, leadership, or the child of dysfunctional parents, spend a greater percentage of resources searching for healing rather than engaging in adventurous plans for the sake of new life. As these cycles spiral deeper and faster, each part reinforces the other. Diminished relationship connections causes the immature to react by inflicting more small cuts. These cuts require greater time away for healing which triggers greater alarm in the immature.

As noted, this scenario is one of the trickiest and most difficult problems in leadership. This is true because the reflexes to find time for healing are the same triggers used by the immature to inflict more and more cuts.

What's a leader to do?

Essentially it is now critical to practice a love of self for the sake of the mission. Since "normal" attempts at appropriate self-management are very difficult to engage, it is critical to take extraordinary measures to find space and time to heal.

In the lives of teenagers caught in these families, the most fortunate will find friendly surrogate extended family. I know a family where the dad is a recovering alcoholic, and as a result of his recovery he has welcomed and mentored children and teens of dysfunctional parents. Although not formally adopted, these teens have been attracted to this family's health. There is conversation where people look each other in the eyes; predictability of interaction, accountability and a spirit of acceptance surround it all. Word of mouth has kept their role as "parents of teens" going for years.

Within the leadership of organizations, the rough equivalent of these mentoring parents is extremely helpful. Finding peers, support groups or professional counsel adds to the healing potential the same way antibiotics intensify the body's response to bacteria. Sabbaticals, leaves of absence and, of course, full change of position are options, but not always feasible. Bringing the whole thing to light usually takes time for the obvious reason – the whole process takes time. Once discovered, however, you can begin to call on spiritual and emotional resources to begin to address what's going on. You want to stay far enough away to protect yourself and those you love. On the other hand you have to find some level of connection to influence for the better.

This means "placing the mask over your own face first." The familiar flight attendant directions are yours. Don't try to overcome too much too quickly. Rather, as much as possible, pull back into a place that feeds your soul. It might be prayer and meditation, Bible readings, your own private worship – whatever it is, even in small ways, find a place to begin to reverse the spiritual depletion – even if it means healing only a few cuts at a time. Secondly, connect, connect, connect. Find a professional counselor, make a date at the end of each day with your spouse, play with children, start an accountability group and meet for breakfast. Relationships will feed you and continue the process God is working within you. Protect, protect, protect. Start the process of organizing routines, boards, people and places to draw boundaries, establish policies, initiate disciplines or simply bring to light the stuff that grows in darkness.

Healing from a disease you didn't know you had takes longer than you think. Give yourself time to engage the healing rhythms to be introduced in the next section. Engage. Disengage. Repeat.

What does this mean?

One of the most difficult resistances to move through is the chronic accumulation of small spiritual and emotional cuts that keep occurring. Because yesterday's pain looks a lot like today's pain, it's easy to lose track of how bad things really are compared to last year at this time. This slow spiraling damage creates a cloak of secrecy that can be far more dangerous than acute stress.

What can you do?

Connecting and protecting are most important. Connect with every friendly face you can. Protect yourself from harm by pulling back as far as you can. Establish regular rhythms of renewal way ahead of time – whether you feel like you need them or not. Because of the slow, imperceptible increase in this deadly stress, you need an oasis set up before hand. Assuming you won't feel a need - do it anyway. Establishing objective wellness markers can save you from the confusing subjectivity that makes you believe you're okay because you felt the same way yesterday. Connect. Connect. Connect. Protect. Protect. Protect.

Lastly
Composed for Rhythm: *Engage. Disengage. Repeat.*

I ask no dream, no prophet ecstasies,
No sudden rending of the veil of clay,
No angel visitant, no opening skies;
But take the dimness of my soul away.

- George Croly
from the hymn, "Spirit of God, Descend Upon My Heart"

Composed for Rhythm is your calling to accept the gift to be fully present in life with extraordinary vitality. Using Jesus' declaration, *"I came that they may have life – and have it abundantly"* this last part of the book, along with the web based tools and resources on KarlGalik.com, will unwrap the gift. (John 10.10) You'll then have opportunity to accept the extraordinary gift of vitality intended for you.

Composed for Rhythm also comes with a warning label, "be aware of the thief" – the thief of your extraordinary vitality. Using Jesus' strong caution, *"The thief comes only to steal and destroy"* this section will begin with stories and examples of such theft. Interestingly enough, it usually looks pretty inviting.

Composed for Rhythm is about the practical integration of our created and designed relationships. Since life itself began in relationship, your life begins and is sustained in relationship and relationship's rhythms.

Chapter 18

Don't Help Others
(To Make Yourself Feel Better)

ᛢᛥᛃ

A busy mother makes slothful daughters.
—Portuguese Proverb

Engage. Disengage. Repeat.

Here is a rhythm that has echoed since Genesis chapter 1.
Engage life. Disengage from life. Repeat the song again.

You are composed to live life according to this simple rhythm.
If you remove any one of these simple steps, life immediately
becomes more difficult. Life also gets unnecessarily more difficult when you overemphasize either of the first two. Typically,
caring people are most likely to over-engage.

Many well-intentioned people mistake exhaustion for Jesus'
invitation to take up your cross and follow him. (Matthew 16.24;
Mark 8.34; Luke 9.23) It is a mistake to think that just because
you're tired that you're doing a noble work. It can actually be irre-
sponsibility dressed up as helpfulness. Whether it is a mom over-
functioning or a dad working too long, a Biblical love of self calls
for times of renewal in order to effectively manage yourself. This
fulfills (not ignores) Jesus' call to take up your cross and follow
him. Doing too much is never enough. There's always more to

do and more you can do – always. It's one of the chief tricks of the Thief.

I recall a conversation I had with a mom of teenage boys. She was exhausted from doing their laundry, fixing all their meals and essentially acting as their personal concierge. "Mom I don't have my favorite jeans to wear." "Mom, can you call my coach for me? I have too much homework to go to practice." The number of sentences, and sentence fragments that began with the word "Mom!" was driving her crazy. Now, I'm sure you can see where this is heading. We all know she was doing everything but managing herself well. She was doing too much for her boys, but it was never enough. She was over-engaging.

The point to capture is deeper than the example. The spiritual and emotional forces operating to seduce her into over-engaging are real and powerful. This woman is intelligent. A computer programmer by trade, she is well read, well spoken and well versed in conversational arts. She is also happily married and of sound mind and body. What pulled her into this place was her love for her boys, her heart for God and a desire to do the right thing. Still, the Thief was robbing her of balanced relationships.

I have seen this in myself as pastor and myriad of times with pastor friends or in coaching consultations. Sharp people, who can't leave a droning meeting early, can't let the ushers fold the bulletins or allow someone else to open the gate to the parking lot on Sunday morning. True story. I once consulted with a congregation for whom the pastor even changed the filters in the furnace. The congregation's request for consultation came after the new pastor had the audacity to refuse this and a myriad of other such responsibilities. In this case, the Thief fleeced everyone because everyone was participating in the over-engaging of the filter-changing pastor.

In another conversation with a group of physicians, there was considerable disagreement regarding who was pulling their weight in the practice. Two were working fairly long and often challenging hours. The third physician was unsatisfied the other two weren't billing the extraordinary time he was. Although his family life was suffering to the point of a pending divorce, he maintained a schedule that left little time for life's relationships. The overworking physician kept working even while his closest relationships were deteriorating before his eyes. What is it that trumps intelligence and common sense? What allows a mom, a pastor, and a physician to be robbed of so much for so little in return?

Over-engaging is actually rooted in self*ishness*. It's the primary tool of the Thief.

Perhaps the over-engaging physician always wanted more work because of the financial reward. Greed can be bred and fed by getting all the stuff you want. Contentment, however, cannot be purchased. It is typically rare and fleeting. The stuff money buys forms its own black hole and blocks out the light with more stuff. Self*ishness* often begins by doing the right thing and then later morphs into doing it for the wrong reason. What begins in moms, pastors, physicians and caring people as self*lessness* decomposes into self*ishness* when the service is no longer for others, but for one's self.

In the midst of emergency surgeries, family crisis or disturbing doubts of faith, pastors can bring the reassuring presence of God to people in need. So, pastors tend to receive reward from a connection to people that covers the full gamut from intervention in difficult times to the joy of baptisms and weddings. The net effect is there are a great many opportunities to have people moving toward pastors for comfort or questions.

It is this combination of finding fulfillment in a relationship vocation and having lots of people moving toward you that can unlock the door for The Thief. The process usually begins in compassion with sincere motives. But somewhere, sometime, caregivers can slip away from being Jesus' presence in the situation, to trying to rescue people from wrestling with their own pain. It's at this point the unlocked door is opened for the Thief.

When caregivers start *rescuing* others from their adversity, instead of ministering to them in their adversity, a subtle shift *begins* to occur. First of all, as any mother who has tried to teach her toddler knows, it's easier to pick the toys up than train the child to do it for herself. In fact, it's exponentially easier.

It is so much easier (to attempt) to rescue or placate the hurting with cliché or religious quips than it is to be truly present in another's fears and doubts. Being present in the pain means being there, coaching or encouraging without resorting to quick fix responses. These shallower responses usually ease the discomfort of the caregiver, but not the person in need. Staying present in the pain is many, many times more difficult than simply spouting quotes or doing a drive-by blessing. It's just easier to see a picked-up room or a full calendar of parishioners than it is to encourage people in adversity to see God's presence through it all. It's much easier to keep a waiting room full of patients than it is to wrestle through issues of intimacy in marriage.

The Thief is looking for the open door to the short cut. Jesus' temptations in the desert were invitations to the short cut. Highly paraphrased and summarized, they may sound like this. "Don't wait to eat, pull over and get something now. (This was the rocks into bread temptation.) Forget about the disciplined life. Instead, throw yourself at life randomly - God will catch you no matter what. (This was the devil's temptation for Jesus to throw himself down off the temple and let God catch him.) Don't suffer for these people because, who really wants to suffer anyway? And, what if it doesn't work?" (This was the temptation to worship the devil instead of trust God that the crucifixion would lead to resurrection.) (Matthew 4.1*f*)

Short cuts of expediency, perhaps a distant relative of multi-tasking, unlatch the door for the Thief. However, the wide-open invitation for the thief to enter comes from "pleasure seeking" as opposed to "mission seeking" motives. For the caregiver, this usually doesn't mean the illicit pleasure seeking of headline fame, but the small serotonin release that comes from being told what a nice person your are; how nice it is you've given up time with your family to be here now. When this mood elevating neurotransmitter comes calling for you, and not for the mission you're on, it is more likely feeding your personal need and devouring your larger calling in the process.

Notice, no crimes have been committed, yet. No moral violation or misconduct has occurred, yet. It's just a nice person responding as a nice person for the wrong reason. In the end, however, it's a short cut to the land of feel good. It's delayed gratification, discipline and trust out the proverbial window – albeit in a very small way. This does not mean a walk with God is not intended to be pleasurable. A walk with God is tremendously pleasurable – but it's the fruit of the relationships that is pleasurable, not the seeking of the pleasure that produces the fruit. It goes like this.

The Thief and his desire for short cuts begins by reminding you of how good it felt last time you helped out. This is a reminder of the sweetness of the fruit of your effort. It naturally felt good to be appreciated for your effort. In the complex interactions of your brain and body, endorphins and little doses of serotonin were released. They produced a sense of satisfaction. The short-cuts of the Thief tempt you to *pursue the feeling* you got from helping out rather than the effort of helping out again. Helping others can get reduced to quick fix pursuits. Clichés replace caring questions. Getting more wealth becomes more important than healing others. Doing the laundry for capable teenagers replaces equipping teens for real life.

The phrase, "Here, let me do that for you" can be courteous. The problem is it can also be a short cut to your own satisfaction. As you take care of your elderly parents, there might be many opportunities for you to open a jar, drag out the hose, or lift a box to a shelf. These are good works and likely to produce the fruit of endorphin-like satisfaction in small doses. Yet, for the elderly person's own good there are likely times when you allow grandma to carry the bucket herself because she needs the effort to maintain healthy bone density and muscle tone. Grandma might look at you funny and wonder why you're being so lazy, when; in fact, you're doing the hard work of loving. Allowing grandma to carry the bucket is your act of love knowing you did right by her even if the in-laws are watching you do nothing. So, the hard work of loving involves doing the right thing even if it means foregoing the momentary feeling of satisfaction.

What's the right thing to do?

The right thing to do is live by grace. Neither you nor I can get these small or larger decisions right each time. They come at us too frequently and in too many forms and scenarios. Attempts to monitor life so closely may lead you to obsessive-compulsive behaviors and create another whole set of problems too complex to define here. No, when you live by grace, you live trusting God's promises, forgiveness and consistent, persistent love for you. It's the relationship of grace itself that finds its home within you, stirs a love within you and leads you to loving decisions. That same life of grace will lead you to loving forgiveness when you make the wrong decision.

Living by grace is first allowing your self to be forgiven and loved. It is next taking that new self and loving others as you have been loved and accepted. Essentially, you have less need for the shortcut, are less tempted by the Thief because you already possess a prevailing sense of satisfaction from knowing you live in grace. As a mom of teens you will begin to trust that the rolled eyes and looks of disgust from teens having to do their own laundry will soon be producing fruits of satisfaction as they successfully begin to organize their own life. As surgeons in a group, living by grace is doing the hard work of love and telling your partner that his share in the business is out of balance with healthy living for everyone else. Living by grace is helping people whenever they're stuck, but perhaps not whenever they want.

Don't say, "Here, let me do that for you." First, think, "What is best for the larger mission here?" Then trust the pursuit of

Godly mission will produce the fruit of satisfaction that tastes so sweet and feels really good!

What does this mean?

Therapists call it "over-functioning." Twelve Step groups call it co-dependence. It's when you are motivated to go the extra mile or two or eight primarily because it feels good at the time – not because it's the right thing to do. Whether or not your help is doing someone else any good is secondary to the feeling you receive when you help. This is one of the earliest places the Thief begins to replace the joy of the mission with selfish joy disguised as helping others.

What can you do?

Ask the question, "Whose need are you meeting?" If you have a hard time answering the question, that's your signal to find someone else to ask it for you. If you discover you're primarily meeting your own needs, you'll next have to decide if you're ready to stop that. Meeting your needs through others is a slippery slope to exhaustion because of the endless needs people can and will present. Partner with others to encourage their mission – not meet your personal needs to be needed.

Chapter 19

The (Welcome) Captivity of Busyness
౼ఌ

Violent passions are formed in solitude.
In the busy world no object has time to make a deep impression.
- Henry Homes (1696-1782)

A second enemy interfering with the *engage, disengage, repeat* rhythm of renewal is addiction. Addiction to drugs and alcohol are well defined and well documented.

What is only now surfacing as a concern is addiction to information so readily available on the Internet. More specifically, the over-pursuit of information shows some of the same harmful relationship symptoms as those addicted to drugs or alcohol. Web sites like Netaddiction.com illustrate the growing epidemic of addiction to information that interferes with everything from work productivity to distracted texting drivers causing accidents. Still far worse than the over-pursuit of information, is the temptation to substitute data for decision-making. This constant digital distraction is present in organizations when leaders choose to take yet another survey or consult another study to the point of needlessly postponing the courage it takes to make bold leadership decisions. In these scenarios, gathering data is more important than gathering together. "Googling" something is easier than asking penetrating questions. This "data addiction" may be the next socially acceptable wave of common addictions – right up there with caffeine and alcohol.

This isn't technology bashing. It is a gospel invitation to use information to inform decisions, not escape them; to glorify God through them instead of consuming information like milk chocolate and always wanting more. This is a call to allow the pursuit of information to follow the same cadence present in the rhythms of renewal. Engage. Disengage. Repeat.

The Bible speaks of the futility of always wanting more information. Consider the introduction to the book of Ecclesiastes,

"He who increases knowledge increases sorrow." (1.18)

The futility of information pursuit is noted in this quote:

" I saw under the sun the race is not to the swift, nor the battle to the strong, nor bread to the wise, nor riches to the intelligent, nor favor those with knowledge, but time and chance happen to them all." (9.11)

St. Paul noted the fleeting value of knowledge over and against the lasting effect of love in at least a few places.

"This knowledge puffs up, but love builds up." (1 Corinthians 8.1)

"Love never ends…as for knowledge, it will pass away." (1 Corinthians 13.8)

For example, increasing sorrow from increased knowledge might be evident when trying to sort through reams of available information about a pending surgery. I've visited with people who were glad to be informed of some of the details of their cancer surgery, but also exasperated by conflicting published opinions. With much knowledge comes much sorrow – in part from the need to discern helpful information from unhelpful, or figuring out how to apply it once you have it. Information does not necessarily provide a formula for making the right decision. The wisdom to apply that knowledge in love, along with just the right timing of circumstance, is as important as the information itself.

Still, the gravest danger is that data addiction robs you of times of renewal. When someone is abusing alcohol, drugs or food, there is tangible evidence, something to point to and say, "It's this vodka that's destroying your soul and the relationships connected to it." With data addiction, it's not so clear. This is true, in part, because information is usually helpful and more information is generally more helpful. Whether you're wondering about the chance of thundershowers prior to a bike ride or estimating the chance your proposal will pass through the meeting, the more specific information you have, the more informed your plans will be. But somewhere on the continuum, more is too much. Other addictions can be defined by some objective information like blood levels, but there is no such medical marker for too much information. Yes, there are physical symptoms from sitting in front of a computer screen too long; eyestrain, stiffness and carpel tunnel. But there are also computer lenses to relax your eyes, ergonomic workstations to assist in proper body posture and surgery to put or keep you back in the know.

Although the amount of information available on a daily basis is exponentially more than what a 15th century man had in lifetime, each informational spike in history has people concerned about its effect on the soul. During the time of the Roman senator and philosopher Seneca, Rome was experiencing the effects of its expansive kingdom with new roads and an elaborate mail system. To that date in history, never before had so much information traveled as far so easily as during the "Peace of Rome." Seneca after he had returned home from a busy day in a bustling crowd said, "I never come back with quite the same moral character I went out with – something or other becomes unsettled."[8]

William Powers, author of *Hamlet's Blackberry* refers to this obsession as an "addiction to distraction."[10]

Although I have to smile at wondering what "moral character" might be lost in a crowd, I also have to confess that I too feel drained after being in crowds all day.

So, whether you are waiting for the mail to arrive from Egypt to Rome, or checking your Droid for texts, while talking to a friend on your drive home, there seems to be little difference in the difficulties of over-connection from Roman to modern times. All too quickly and invisibly a line is crossed and you find yourself somewhere between depleted and suffering some loss of moral character. Across the centuries there is a human inclination for stimulation that sooner or later interferes with health and well being.

No matter the era or culture, the greatest danger is in avoiding the *disengage* rhythm. If you memorized the complex formula for renewal; *engage, disengage, repeat*, you'll recall this is number two of three. God's design, even illustrated by his own practice of resting on the Sabbath, magnifies the necessity for the pattern of renewal. Without the *disengage* part, you go right to the *repeat* part and are caught in an endless loop of *engage, repeat, engage, repeat, ad infinitum*. It might look familiar to you. It might feel familiar to you. It might be the thing damaging your moral character, like it did Seneca when he lingered in Roman crowds.

Although all addictions captivate, few, if any do so with the subtlety of busyness in the pursuit of information. Although any activity that seduces you to skip the *disengage* part is a problem, the pursuit of more and more data scratches an itch shared by most everyone. The universality of the addiction to data, or "addiction to distraction" is its secret power. By diminishing and eventually interrupting the renewal rhythm, life itself is interrupted or diminished. In the extreme, you know what sleep deprivation would do to you in a matter of days. Well, just call it "information" or "knowledge" or "connection" and watch it do the same thing – just a lot more slowly. The difference between sleep deprivation and over-connection to data is its cultural acceptance in ancient Rome or modern Chicago. Sleep deprivation will drive you crazy pretty quickly. Over-connection will do the same thing – just a lot more slowly. Instead of a piercing wound on the soul from abusing narcotics, information over-pursuit is like scratching the soul till it bleeds, a little. And, lest it heal, it is scratched a little more the next day, on and off all day till it interferes with sleep that night.

This is why Jesus invites us to a new and different "yoke." The burden of love that a Christian life provides discovers passion that includes *disengaging* for the purpose of further engaging. In the same way a tough coach works his players hard and then provides recovery time, so the Spirit leads to a rhythm best for loving and leading others. There are plenty of things to learn, but also time to let it go, for now. There's plenty of work to do, but always time for children and a shared meal. There's plenty of time for working long, hard hours – occasionally to the point of exhaustion. Then there's time away for a quiet place, still waters with bread and wine.

Instead of ordering a pizza online, try gathering with family and friends and making pizzas from scratch. Instead of playing games online, try playing Uno with your parents. Instead of researching your next dream vacation online, begin with sitting on the couch together sharing a cup of hot chocolate and imagining the place where you'd like to be together and then find the best deal online (later). Instead of going to Web M.D., first, try sitting with the person who is ill and praying for their recovery. Instead of creating a midi file on your laptop, sing an acoustic love song to your girlfriend. Disengage from the impersonal and create the personal.

Rather than being held captive to busyness, the "yoke" of Jesus captivates you in a productive refreshing rhythm. Engage. Disengage. Repeat.

What does this mean?

It's impossible to have enough information. It's not possible to complete all you've ever wanted to do. There's always something else to keep you busy or more information to be gained about another subject. Busyness can be welcomed as an excuse to avoid disengaging. Busyness disrupts the rhythms of renewal for which you are designed. It substitutes distraction for productivity.

What can you do?

Disengage. The only way to disengage is to disengage. Consider rest as management of your personal energy. Set boundaries for yourself on how long you'll return emails or clean the house. Practice saying, "No, I'm not too busy to…" and then fill in the blank with a relationship or activity. Recognize that the goal is to create a time when you're not too busy to enjoy the company of family and friends.

Chapter 20

How Can A Burden Provide Rest?

"Come to me...and I will give you rest"
- Jesus (Matthew 11.28*f*)

I f you've ever felt fatigue and satisfaction at the same time, then you get it. If you've ever finished a triathlon and walked over to the display board to see when and where the next race will be held, you understand. If you've ever felt relief after you've spent most of the night rocking a sick and restless infant to sleep, fighting sleep and exhaustion yourself, then you already know what this chapter is about. It is an exploration of Jesus' invitation to engage the rest he has in mind.

> *Come to me, all who labor and are heavy laden, and I will give you rest. Take my yoke upon you, and learn from me, for I am gentle and lowly in heart, and you will find rest for your souls. For my yoke is easy, and my burden is light.* - Jesus (Matthew 11.28-30)

Although life with Jesus is deeply engaging, it also supplies rest for your soul. Although a life of Christian discipleship may drain you of energy, you will also experience high levels of satisfaction that recharge your batteries to full. Although there are certainly times when you will exert yourself to your limits, you will be refueled in spirit, by the Spirit who has infinite resource.

Because he is both God and human, Jesus has complete understanding of how your love can over-function and act in selfish ways instead of serving others in selfless ways. He too has been tempted to start down this path to burnout and frustration. He too has journeyed down this back alley to wits end.

Because he became human while remaining Divine, he also knows of your unhealthy needs to be over connected…always seeking more and more even though it delivers less and less. Jesus was tempted with "addictions to distraction" as we are. He practiced a rhythm of engaging; teaching his disciples, healing the sick, challenging the arrogant leaders or circulating in the crowds. Then He disengaged. He escaped to a quiet place, went to the next town or got up dark and early to be with his Dad, alone. He had eleven followers who didn't get it for the longest time. He had one follower who never got it. He had a global mission to ignite. Yet, instead of working 24/7, he exercised his Father's rhythms of renewal to engage, disengage and repeat.

This chapter is a Biblical blueprint for renewal for the purpose of joining Jesus' mission. His missions may leave you as spent as the triathlon athlete at the finish line, but he will also provide rest - and a deeply seated desire to do it again! The combination of profound purpose engaged with natural rhythms of renewal is the yoke of delight, and the burden that gives you joy to bear. This was a daily journey Jesus himself employed in order to accomplish in three years what would change the world forever. That you may find rest for your soul – that your soul might fully engage after resting is the nature of the yoke and burden Jesus provides.

The renewal Jesus provides comes as an invitation that is called a "gospel imperative." At first blush it looks like the two words don't belong together. On the one hand the Gospel is all about what Jesus did for you, his great and unconditional love for you. The Gospel is not a command to be religious or any kind of command at all. It's an invitation within a proclamation. It's someone knocking at the door. It beckons to be opened, but you don't have to answer it. You aren't commanded or pressured to open it. That's the gospel, the Good News of a great gift waiting on the other side of the door – for you.

But in this Bible verse this invitation is paired with an "imperative." An imperative is a command. It's something you've got to do. So, when you put these words together it's a little bit like oil and vinegar. You can shake it up to mix it up, but give it some time and the two will naturally segregate right there in the bottle. So it is with the oil of "gospel" and the vinegar of "imperative." They appear together in their unnatural shaken up state to communicate a specific and special message, called the gospel imperative – Good News you simply must hear!

Marilouise, my beloved for more than three decades, may be the master of the gospel imperative. Albeit in many and varied forms, and at as many places you might not expect just such an invitation - she is there to offer it. When we dine together, she often offers gospel invitations. "Hmm, umm, y*ou've got to try a bite of this.*" Even when I, or others with whom we're sharing a meal politely decline, her fork continues to be thrust over the invitational plate with insistence. She's certain if I miss this taste, life, as I'm experiencing it over my own plate, will not be as rich.

I smirk, then smile, give her "that look" then, enjoy her offering. I'm usually glad I did. Sometimes the joy comes with the anticipated taste, but it always comes with her invitation to me! It's one of the things I love about her – the way she engages even the most simple of pleasures with full embrace.

A few years ago, we went to see the Body Worlds exhibit. Plasticized bodies in different postures, exposing and illustrating the complicated systems of the body, were everywhere. Marilouise's physical therapy studies and love for her work brought on such enthusiasm, she turned out to be an informal, passionate tour guide for an impromptu small group. By the time we got to illustrations of the sciatic nerve, people were nodding in unison. *"Look here, this is why the pain runs down your leg..."* We *had* to see it. We were all glad we did! I gave her that look, but she didn't notice; she was on to the next fascinating exhibit.

> *"Come to me all who labor and are heavy laden and I will give you rest."*
> - Jesus (Matthew 11.28)

Jesus invites, but he does so with the joy of Marilouise and a fork full of delight. If you'll allow extrapolation beyond interpretation, Jesus might be saying, *"You've got to come to me! I really, really want you to come to me. I know what it's like to taste and see how I am good. I know what it's like to look and see what delights I have in store. You will learn, heal and grow - if you will please come to me!"*

As you experience Jesus' invitations, so you too are likely to get all "imperative" in your invitation. It begins with Jesus' provision, and continues with your taste and experience. It's likely you can recommend a good double chocolate cake because it looks good, but it will lack the passionate enthusiasm, the "hmm, umm" vocals if you don't taste it first. You'll discover Jesus' gospel invitations always come with joy because his invitation is to you, for the joys of eternity he has already tasted.

In comparing/contrasting different English translations you can get a pretty solid sense of the essence of this passage.

> *"Come to me, all you who are weary and burdened, and I will give you rest."* —NIV

> *"Come to me all who labor and are heavy laden, and I will give you rest."* — ESV

> *"Are you tired? Worn out? Burned out on religion? Come to me. Get away with me and you'll recover your life. I'll show you how to take a real rest."* — The Message

Although The Message is an interpretation, rather than a translation, you can sense Eugene Peterson's effort to bring out the context and urgency of Jesus' Gospel invitation.

"Come" Imperative, second person plural, active. Here's the urgent calling. If you're similar to Marilouise and love to share experiences that stir you, then you certainly are likely to understand the tone and voice of Jesus. "Come" might be expanded to say, "Come on…" or "What are you waiting for…" All of this is likely to be accompanied by hand gestures of beckoning, encouraging, waving or extending. "You've got to try this."

"Weary" Present tense participle, in other words it could be pressed to say, *"you in the process of wearing down…"*

"You, weary from stepping into suffering through life's draining circumstances…" like moms taking care of sick or handicapped children, Dads getting up to restart the in-home chemotherapy for their 12 year old daughter, or children with diabetes monitoring glucose levels.

You, weary from working 50, 60, 70, hour weeks…." like the single mom with two jobs struggling through a bad economy, the high school girl who needs to study twice the time of her sister, or the nearly retired employee working to save before mandatory retirement age.

"You, weary from trying to be there for everybody…" like nurses on a twelve hours shift attending to two or three call buttons at once; like you ready to pull your hair out if you hear one more, "Mom can I have…" You going to work you hate on a shift you can't stand with people who are hard and crude.

"You, weary to the point of running dry, running out of steam, running…" because you feel like you're just going through the motions. You're so tired, so sick and tired of being the butt of racial slurs and ethnic comments, so emotionally fatigued from watching your spouse slowly kill himself and daily making the family pay the price of vigilance for alcoholism.

Any or all of these illustrate the way in which the pursuit of life is wearing you down like sandpaper against a harsh surface.

These, and far too many more examples are inherent in Jesus' call, *"Come! You the one in the process of wearying..."* from the energy it takes just to get through one more day.

Jesus next targets the nature of chance, the evil and randomness that comes your way like a drunken driver crossing over the double yellow line.

"Burdened" Perfect passive participle, i.e., "you in the process of being burdened..."

"You, in the process of being burdened by other's suffering..." such as the nurse in the children's oncology ward, or the firefighter carrying out an elderly woman with third degree burns; or the foreman tasked with laying off the person you know is already at financial wits end.

"You, in the process of being burdened by fatigue..." such as the early-rising fisherman getting up before dawn and going to work – then changing clothes and going to his bartending job. You, the parent reaping the fatigue from not teaching your children respect and boundaries in their early elementary years, and now having to discipline disrespectful teens. Or you, the woman in need of total knee replacement waiting on tables and counting the hours till the shift is over.

"You, in the process of being burdened by always being 'on'" like the pastor who's grocery shopping and stopped in the bread aisle to be chastised for the wrong music in worship; or the child of an alcoholic mom who has to always pretend things are fine at home.

"You, in the process of feeling pulled in multiple directions without time to focus..." like the parents of triplets who all became "viable eggs' when fertilized; like the man attending to his wife's chronic struggle with lupus while his daughter causes a car accident; or like the man whose sewer backed up the morning of his daughter's wedding.

"You, in the process of being burdened by fear of the unknown..." of what will happen when your company gets bought out. Your fears may circulate around what may happen in retirement if your

IRA continues to diminish. You may feel the burden of what to do now that your girlfriend is pregnant and you just applied to medical school.

This litany of real life issues is intended to illustrate the wide-ranging potential for Jesus' invitation of those actively wearing down by dealing with life, and those passively being worn down because of life's abrasive rubbing between the world, the flesh and the devil. The yoke and burden of Jesus for rest encompasses both that which you are doing, and that which is happening to you.

"Rest." First person, future, active *"I will cause you to cease, to rest..."* Like a mother calming a fearful child with a loving embrace, so Jesus is the author of your calm. A relationship with him means you can have assurance in the midst of trials in the same way a pilot calms passengers flying through turbulence. Yes, it's bumpy, but no, it's not dangerous when you're buckled in. So, the "rest" Jesus provides comes from trusting that he's in control and provides assurance that life's turbulence is temporary. Staying buckled up to his truth means you feel the bumps, but you know they aren't going to hurt you.

Yes, some problems you gave to yourself. Other trials simply happened to you because of the nature of the world in which we live. But either way, the gospel imperative is for you. Regardless of who started it, where it came from or how it happened, you are secure in his insistence you come to him to discover it has already been taken care of. This is the gospel message. God loved, so God gave.

This is the imperative message. You've simply *got* to respond. Answer the door. Open your heart and trust. The yoke and burden of Jesus may tire you out from time to time, but it will always refresh you beyond imagination. It will always taste richer than you thought. It will always leave you ready to join Marilouise in insisting that the people you love try some too!

What does this mean?

The "yoke" and "burden" of Jesus invites you to a life lived for what really matters. Whether you call it "purpose-driven" or Godly living, it's like the burden of raising a child. It cost you dearly, but gives back richness to the soul. The burden of Jesus is the burden of work that is naturally produced when you love someone. When it goes well, loving is hard work you enjoy doing!

What can you do?

Strive to invest in significance that is often found in relationship. Look for purpose that will usually be defined by improved lives of others. Invest in those things that have eternal consequences, lasting importance. Invest in those things that matter to God. Those things always give back more than you put in.

Chapter 21

Surrender and Renewal
are Inseparable

Leisure should be a time to think new thoughts, not ponder old ills.
—C. Neil Strait, Leader in the Church of the Nazarene

Disengaging is harder than it seems. Although the idea of disengaging seems inviting, the actual doing of it happens far less than the dream. The beer commercial on the beach makes it look inviting, but the act of setting aside time and money hinders more people than it invites. The passing fantasy of solitude is welcoming, but powering off the smart phone for a day may seem insurmountable.

Deep down, letting go for a while is really a spiritual issue more than it is a time management one. There is something about letting go that alarms the human spirit. "What ifs?" spring up and attack trust. Yet, without the desire and ability to "let go" you become weary and worn out. Surrender and renewal really require trust building in one's relationship to God and one another for the purpose of disengaging.

God is God and I am not.

The ancient illustration of this is found in the original sin of Adam and Eve's decision to take matters into their own hands. Their distrust of God has been faithfully reproduced in humanity ever since. People don't like to be blamed for someone's sin long ago, but then reflexively make selfish decisions. (Genesis 3.1-8) The devil's evil innuendo is a crafty way to insert doubt where only trust existed. *"Did God really say…?"* It is a subtle but powerful tool. It is a colorless, odorless, tasteless but toxic fume. The toxic gas smells like this. *"Does she really have the right motives?"* As trust is infiltrated, it begins to slowly break down into a fog-like state of wondering about possibilities. *"Do you really know where your wife goes when she leaves the office?"* The oxygen of assurance is inconspicuously dissipated with a flammable gas that's just dying to explode. *"Did God actually say?"*

If someone has unfairly raised doubts about you, then you have felt the destructive force of such gaseous, toxic build-up. These damaging questions act like a toxic gas to harm you and those close to you. When a spark of accusation ignites the innuendo fumes, relationships blow up. Boom - followed by shock, surprise, ducking and running. Usually its not the person or the people who filled the room with explosive gases of doubt that are blamed. Rather, blame is typically placed on the one who threw a spark from all the emotional friction building up. It's not unlike the abused wife syndrome. Because the rising tension from the abusive husband may go on for days, weeks, even months, a wife finally looks for relief from the escalating emotional flammable gases by throwing a spark. She commits some "violating" rigid demand designed to maintain her fear. Then suddenly the "explosion" occurs.

I have visited with these women who have been exhausted by the tension-building phase, and out of love for themselves, or their children "take the blame" by throwing a spark. In effect this declares her refusal to live another day breathing toxic relationship gases. I have gained a special place within my own heart for these women who find it hard to take a breath of fresh air in their own homes.

Within organizations, people in leadership often fill the spark-throwing role. Changing rhythms and routines that alter direction can produce enough friction to throw a spark into any gaseous mix of doubt or innuendo. I recently spoke with a high school principal who had to make some very difficult staff decisions. Within days Facebook was used to fill the high school hallways with toxic innuendo gasses. Within organizations of all types, innuendos get dressed up as "orthodoxy" designed to maintain familiar rhythms and routines. Those representing "the way it has always been" often resort to toxic-fume building questions to undermine new direction. Listen for such things as, "Does he know what he's doing?" or "Who does she think she is?" These questions are just like turning on a natural gas valve and allowing it to pour into the hallways of an organization. People smell something foul, but seldom call attention to what's happening.

The result is the same in marriages or any organization. When a spark of conflict ignites the fumes, the innuendo shrapnel damages surrender and trust. Relationships no longer provide a place of rest or refreshment. They drain rather than fulfill you. Defenses remain at high alert, over-revving the soul, working hard at remaining vigilant for noxious fumes of innuendo that cannot easily be detected. Ceaseless vigilance rather than cease-less praying (1 Thessalonians 5.16) becomes the norm.

So, you might feel the tension in the marriage, but not know how to describe it. You may sense the uneasiness within leader-ship, but not be able to put your finger on why you can't relax. You might participate in awkward conversations at the office, but the slow and gradual build up of toxic fumes has the same slowly life damaging effect as "death by a thousand cuts." In the begin-ning, you can't tell what you're sensing or describe what you're feeling. You just know it's not right. You start looking for ways to avoid being around it.

Such is the insidious nature of original sin, and its effect on relationships and refreshment over time. It interrupts the *engage, disengage, repeat* rhythms of renewal. Shortness of breath, anxiety about the future, and fear of the unknown are natural responses to pending explosions. You've been designed with the fight or flight response built into your psyche. What the original forces of doubt do is attempt to trigger that response to *perceived* threat – instead of real threat. Concerns about what might happen flood your mind and wash away space to disengage. It is usually easier to get away from real threat than perceived threat. A real threat, like someone throwing rocks at you, propels you in fight of flight mode. However, if the noxious fumes of doubt and fear are only perceived, that means they reside in your head and they go where you go. No sense running away – they will be there wherever you go.

So, refreshment is denied because relaxing, surrendering or letting go are sacrificed to the evil innuendo producing toxic, flammable but invisible gasses. Surrender and refreshment are first cousins because they have the same genetic code for renewal. Refreshment, real and lasting renewal is so elusive, in part, because of its relationship to surrendering all the fears we have to let go of in order the appreciate it.

Fortunately there are elements of surrender built into many of our routines that leads to the refreshment we need. The important renewal of sleep requires a "drifting off" to be supported by your bed. Even a good night of uninterrupted sleep comes from releasing your cares of the day – the origin of bedtime prayers. Military commanders create perimeters, and establish "green zones" where the tremendous vigilance of guards is sacrificed in order to provide rest for the other soldiers. It's important for you to have your own green zones for emotional relief as well. One such "green zone" for me during a particularly trying time was a small group of men I met for breakfast every Thursday morning. Their counsel and friendship were valuable, but just as valuable was the space that was created to allow me to speak and feel freely. Trusting your partner or a true friend with your personal inner life connects you to something other than your fears. True friendships or intimate marriages are described as a place to "just let go and be you."

It seems everything from surgery to flying requires surrender and trust. All the while it remains one of the highest hurdles for the human spirit to climb over. In order to find time for surrender in increasingly connected digital lives, more people are searching for ways to surrender up their souls – if even for a short time. The rise in the popularity of yoga classes, the mainstreaming of biofeedback training, and even the interest in sensory deprivation tanks demonstrates something about the human spirit trying to surrender in order to refresh. One sensory deprivation advertisement I found promised relief from neck and back pain. Meditation, relaxation and even enlightenment are advertised to be found in "floating" or sensory deprivation.

Because all of life comes down to the ultimate surrender of death, all of life's surrendering is but practice for the ultimate time to trust and let go. Death focuses the point of this chapter with laser-like precision. At last, in death one thing is ultimately true – God is God and you're not. Thank God!

Secondly, because these small and large surrendering rehearsals of life are woven together with renewal, so the gift of renewed life is woven into ultimate renewal. Each surrendering experience in life tastes a little like a small piece of the prime rib before it is served at the banquet. (1 Corinthians 15.42f) All of life's surrendering rehearsals are a foretaste of the banquet to come. Getting lost in great music, being absorbed by a backyard hammock, reveling in putting on a plush robe after a hot shower are all fleeting hints of the letting go experienced in eternity with God.

The culture becomes a mosaic of each of our desires to "not surrender" because at the heart of it, people are still wrestling with whether they can be God or not. You keep hearing, "*Did God actually say…*" and sometimes repeat it to others if they seem too peaceful. Between the voices in your head that want life the way you pictured it, and the evil innuendos from angry and hurting people, they work together to create a culture of self-centered doubt. So marketers and business ventures make it a priority for it to be all about you – in a selfish way.

The problem, of course, is that when it is all about you, the link between surrender and refreshment is lost to an endless pursuit for elusive pleasure. Ironically, the cost of reaching for God-like status is to never rest, to never be renewed. It amounts to having your humanity worn down to an unrecognizable nub in pursuit of trying to become God-like. Perhaps this was the primary fear of the original brother Cain who was afraid of becoming a "restless wanderer" outside the presence of God. (Genesis 4.14) Perhaps this is the larger story of the people of Israel restlessly wandering in the desert for forty years. (Deuteronomy 8.2) Perhaps this is the larger story still of our restless wandering magnified by jumping from one fad to another - one quick fix pursuit after another. We love to wander. We're easily distracted.

The Bible's story is about undoing the original evil innuendo question, *"Did God actually say…"* and replacing it with, *"Yes, God did actually say don't eat of the tree in the middle and I trust he has his reasons."* This allows a total surrender to God. It allows you to roll your eyes at the foolish accusation of another. Jesus identified this surrender in the imagery of a farmer.

> *"… unless a grain of wheat falls into the earth and dies, it remains alone; but if it dies, it bears much fruit."* – Jesus (John 12.24)

St. Paul followed suit,

> *"You foolish person! What you sow does not come to life unless it dies."*
> - St. Paul (1Corinthians 15.36)

Surrender is as simple as planting a seed and watching it grow. But it also seems difficult because every seed you plant gets buried out of sight and is out of your control.

Jesus did much more than teach this surrender in farmer's metaphor - he fully engaged it. Why did Jesus cry, *"My God Why Have You Forsaken Me?"* Jesus surrendered to the Father's will well beyond the physical brutality of the cross. He surrendered to the Father's will well beyond the betrayals and denials and fleeing of trusted companions. He surrendered to the very depths of abandonment of hell itself – and trusted the Father would bring him back. This is the heart of the Gospel message. It provides as a gift what Jesus has done for you that you could not do for yourself. It is the lasting assurance that surrender and refreshment are not only linked together now, but will be forevermore. It is the promise that renewal will come if you'll but let go. It is the gift of God's grace realized in the familiar cliché, let go and let God. It is the motive and Spirit-driven-power to let go now.

Trust me.

There will always be those in your organization or perhaps even your family who are well practiced in the innuendo, *"Did God really say..."* Like the original Tempter, it is likely they themselves are restless wanderers looking for company in their misery. Their purpose is to make you afraid to surrender to keep you from the renewal God intends – both now and in the Life to come. God's design is to empower you to simply receive what has already been won for you. All you have to do is surrender and you'll be refreshed and renewed. That's the good news.

What does this mean?

The practice of disengaging requires "letting go." The problem is that "letting go" is one of the most challenging spiritual exercises on the planet. It is against natural human inclination to let go and trust. On top of that, toxic gaseous doubts about God are emitted that cause us to fear letting go. Yet without "letting go" it is impossible to *disengage*. The result is a lifestyle without time for rest and renewal that makes you easily distracted, aimless wanderers. Engaging life's rhythms of renewal calls for spiritual surrender. In *The Love Paradox* surrender actually provides more control.

What can you do?

Let go. Practice letting go in spiritual ways. Pray often and end each prayer with the phrase, "Your will be done." Ask for forgiveness. Give a heartfelt apology; look someone in the eye and ask him or her to forgive you (like Jesus forgave them). Let go in emotional ways by trusting people with just enough responsibility, knowing they may fail, but not so much that they're bound to fail. Let go by laughing out loud more. Delegate housework and anticipate it won't get done the way you have imagined it. Let go in spiritual-financial ways by returning the tithe of God's gift to you, so that He can bless all you have. Let go physically by going to bed each night with gratitude for what you do have. Let go of busyness by finding times to switch off all electronics. If you have to start in five-minute increments and go from there, do it. Practice letting go.

Chapter 22

Composed for Rhythm:
Engage. Disengage. Repeat.
ॐ

For everything there is a season, and a time for every matter under heaven.
- King Solomon (Ecclesiastes 3.1)

Engage

First God created, then he connected.

From the very beginning, the created and connected required caring.

The Lord God took the man and put him in the Garden of Eden to work and to keep it." (Genesis 2.15) The ancient Hebrew verb is in the infinitive form, *"to work."* This means that with the creation of humanity, there is anticipated expenditure of energy. There's work to be done here in this created place. The purpose of placement in the garden is to tend it. It's as if Adam were told, "Here, work it, then watch it respond to you and you to it." The original elements of Paradise are: God's presence, relationship and purposeful effort. God is in full communion with humanity. Relationship is established, and purposeful effort is provided *"in the garden of Eden to work and to keep it."* There is a powerful sense of significance. Adam matters.

This ancient text provides insight into the nature of the Designer's design. It offers insight into the nature of your nature, the core of your being and your need for purpose and significance. You're created from the ground up to engage. It is built into your spirit and your DNA. Your muscles need effort to maintain and exhaustion to grow. Your bones need to bear weight to maintain or gain density. Movement enhances blood flow.

So, from the beginning, you've been created, connected and called *to care* for the whole thing. Everything about you is designed to be in motion and engaged. Your senses are designed to be in motion, assimilating information and interacting with the environment. When that is denied you quite literally can go crazy from isolation. You've been designed to be in relationship. If you can't be in relationship, you'll also go crazy from the loneliness. Like everything else in the garden, your relationships need to be tended to grow. Working and tending the garden also involves tending to the relationships God provides. Paradise was intentionally designed with relationships and purposeful work that need engaging.

Perhaps you already know what happens when relationships stagnate. There are physical symptoms that develop from interpersonal troubles. Emotional stress settles in and influences immune resiliency, emotional stamina and physical wellbeing. In the case of stuck marriages with children at home, for example, the children become accustomed to interacting in a stagnant emotional environment. In fact, the emotional environment in the home impacts their development. That, in turn, influences mate selection, which in turn, affects any children born to the next generation in marriage. Stuck relationships have intergenerational impact. The connecting Creator intended relationships to be tended, or they can have a negative effect for generations.

So, the design for engaging life is clear. First God created, then he connected. Next came the gift of purposeful living by caring, tending and nurturing the gifts provided. Paradise is for engaging and being a part of the creative interaction that produces new life.

The break down in this new engaging life comes when these relationship connections are severed.

When the tending of relationships begins to break down, engagement is slowly replaced by a hypnotic dormancy sometimes called the status quo. In a gradual decline, desire and passion are replaced with reluctance, anxiety or out and out fear. There are limitations and fears that are always calling you back to a sleepy satisfaction for the status quo. You like things the way they are. You might even imagine liking them the way they were. The primary creed of this sleepy satisfaction is, "It's good enough."

One of the primary enemies of managing your new self well is this hypnotic stagnation, this heavy reluctance to engage life. An aversion to engage is the natural inclination of the human spirit after all the original gifts were ruined. St. Paul compares it to the anesthetizing of a drunken stupor. (1Corinthians 15.34) Alcoholics have repeatedly taught me that anesthetizing, although good for surgery, is a problem for engaging real life. Life usually gets worse while you are off somewhere anesthetizing yourself.

Waking up is hard to do. Engaging life means being woken up to the urgency of a gospel invitation. Go! Let everyone know they're free! Come! Let everyone know they can let go, surrender and take a break. The urging of the gospel invitation is now necessary to engage life in the deepest sense because once the original design was ruined; the engaging became a chore, instead of a natural desire.

Waking up is hard to do because it seems there are always weeds to pull, and thorns and thistles to rub up against that pinch and prick. And, worse yet, all you have to do is nothing – and more weeds encroach. Doing nothing is not helpful option, but doing something is hard to do.

The Good News is that the penalty for what has been ruined has been paid. This is what the crucifixion was for. This is why Jesus cried out, *"My God my God why have you forsaken me?"* (Matthew 27.46) The Good News is that in the meantime, before you return to the original design of Paradise, the Spirit of God replenishes the spirit that wants to roll over and mutter, "What's the use?" This is what the resurrection is for. It means you and what you do once again matters. Dead ends open up and become passages through difficulty. The weight of despair is transformed into temporary disappointments. The Good News is that Jesus restores the ruined relationships by renewing and washing clean everything from the forgiveness he offers. The Good News is that he places you back in community – the way you were origi-nally designed – free – separate but connected.

When people complain that religion isn't practical, I point them to people who know they are free. These are people unen-cumbered by wondering if they measure up or can keep up the pace much longer. When spiritually free people get caught up in the rat race, they know there's an exit ahead for them. And, if they miss that one, there's another after that. Without it being license to be lazy and stay in the rat race, it supplies confidence there is a place to exit, to surrender and start again in the morning. The empty tomb on Easter means that efforts at tending the garden will pay off, even though it can often be frustrating. It means imperfect relationships here will be perfect relationships in eternity. It means you have a freedom that allows you to make mistakes.

So, with engagement restored by the gospel, you might think engagement is a way of life. Not so fast. With engagement restored, comes the necessity for disengagement. Remember, you've been composed for rhythm. The gospel imperative calls you to a rhythm of grace. Engage. Disengage. Repeat.

Disengage

It is agreed by many both in and outside of Christian circles that life rapidly exploded into being. Without detouring into the evolution versus intelligent design debates, I personally equate the explosion of life with God's Word being spoken. The Spirit hovered and his presence brought something *ex nihilo* (Latin for *"out of nothing"*). He then organized it, gave it boundaries, definition and purpose. God speaks up and stuff happens.

Now at the risk of sacrilege, I've had to wonder how taxing that really was, how hard a day that could really be. If the vibrations of God's voice start the universe vibrating with life, how draining could that have possibly been? If "nothing" responds and becomes "something" organized and useful, they had to be pretty compelling and commanding words from a compelling and commanding God.

After all the interrelationships fit together; after he had revealed the pinnacle of creation as a male-female couple made in his image - he rested. He took a *Sabbath* (the Hebrew word used twice in Genesis 2.2). Questions naturally arise. Can or does God actually get tired? Well, it doesn't say he got tired. In that verse, the Bible says God was "finished" so he stopped. The simplicity is disarming. But, later, in the very next Biblical book of Exodus, it does say that there was a result from God's Sabbath. "He was refreshed." (Exodus 31.17) Sabbath, it seems, is a sacred rest from engaging and is designed to happen not so much because you're tired, but because you're finished. The result of Sabbath is refreshing. Can God take a break? Here the Bible, starkly simple, doesn't say he needed a rest. It just says He was finished. So, he created a Sabbath, and then took one. He was refreshed by it. God either liked it so much, or foresaw you would need it so much; he set it aside to be used like the good china – roughly 16% of the time.

This original pattern seems to say you're designed to engage and everything is designed to respond to your engagement, so you'll need to run at optimum. In this you will find larger purpose. So, here's what you do. Eight-four percent of the time engage, but then be finished. Sixteen percent of the time take a *Sabbath*. Cease from engaging for sixteen percent of the time. Be finished. You have approximately five times the space and time to engage, so, you'll have plenty of engagement opportunity. The purpose of Sabbath is to be ready to engage the other eighty-four percent of the time.

Nowhere does God say a Sabbath is punishment. Nowhere does he set it up as a "time out" given to children who disobey. I can't find anywhere in the Bible where God waves his hand in disgust and says, oh, just go take a Sabbath! Yet, when a Sabbath is introduced into life today, the sounds from the group are like people being instructed in self-mutilation techniques. There are groans as if being punished. I've had wellness workshop scheduled for organizations that postponed them because they were too busy and there was strife and discontent within leadership. I've had staff share their aggravation with me when I hosted "mandatory" Sabbatical Days. Some were agitated because I arranged for a day away from the office when they had all this work to do. A "Sabbatical Day" was a continental breakfast, relaxed conversation, a devotional, and discussion around a larger question such as "How have you experienced God lately?". That discussion led to some conversation about their work and ministry. I usually asked how I could encourage their efforts. It concluded with a very nice lunch. People were asked not to go back to work, but to head out and do something they enjoyed for a few hours.

There it is. The same people who might be most blessed were often most likely to avoid the opportunity. A few attended, but looked at me with that "I'm only here because I have to be" look. One used it as a forum to complain. These same responses and scenarios are played out in the fields of medicine, counseling, and work environments throughout corporate America. When I do "First Manage Yourself Well" workshops, there's usually a lament heard from the group that I don't really understand how incredibly busy people they really are.

From my training as a therapist, I've learned this is also the song sung in most early counseling sessions. People often arrive for counseling eager to convince the counselor why their dysfunction is so necessary. There is no doubt that crunch time happens. There is also no doubt that when crunch time becomes lifetime, the downward spiral has begun. Physical, mental, emotional and spiritual health all decline when crunch time becomes lifetime. When the rhythm for which you've been composed is lost to the drone of busyness, you suffer; the people around you suffer; and the mission of your organization is diminished.

Why all the pain and suffering around disengaging? At least in small part, it may be because it can slowly sneak up on you one smart phone upgrade at a time. With each upgrade comes the ability to be more connected to more work more often. However, it can be a bit more problematic than that. I believe it has as its roots in the addiction to data addressed earlier. Even deeper than addiction to data, it has roots in ultimately what all addictions are – failure to live in that original trusting relationship with God.

To be curious is healthy, but to have more information instantaneously available than you could possible digest in a lifetime may be like putting a hungry child in an ice cream store. You can fill yourself up with all the flavors you can eat, but it's likely you'll get sick and certain you'll not be getting what you really need to be healthy. Gathering data can become more important than gathering for prayer. Multi-tasking is mastered at the cost of quiet presence.

What I find lacking in much of the health and wellness research is that it does not address the original, deeper resistance to disengage. It does not address the original pursuit for god-like status that ruined everything in the first place. All the information in the world regarding what's appropriate for health and fitness will be ignored or distained as long as it calls on you to spiritually surrender.

Ultimately, the natural rhythms of renewal are not found in trying harder or going faster. They are found in surrender. A time of surrender leads to gratitude rather than quick fix pursuits that lead to a kind of slavery. When you are ready to trust your life to the God who created you, and wants you back, you are then, and only then, ready to fully disengage. The process and act of disengaging is a deeply spiritual process to trust, let go and get caught up in the rhythm for which you have been composed. This is why I understand the nature of conversion as God's loving action for you. You can't let go of the rope and catch yourself at the same time.

Repeat

The rhythms of renewal have their power in what they are - Gospel invitations to receive the rhythm of life in its original design. Someone has to initiate sound for you to hear it. When that someone initiates sound, it resonates within you. "And God said, '*Let there be…and there was.*" (Genesis 1) God, the Great Initiator, began to speak and the universe began to resonate. A scholarly professor, talented composer, and personal friend helped me understand music as purposefully organized sound. Since the universe is purposefully organized, it makes me wonder whether perhaps God sang creation into existence. Is it the stuff of poets to imagine God's voice as song vibrating and exciting life from nothing?

People smarter than me have proposed a mathematically complex hypothesis regarding the smallest of matter. Some scientists call this the study of superstring theory, stating that the smallest matter arises from the excitation of a "string" that has "zero mass and two units of spin."[11] So, life, as poets and scientists have come to know it, seems to be organized into purposeful vibrations. And since rhythm is the movement of sound through time, the matter around us carries the Song sung from the beginning when the Initiator caused his voice to resonate in the created universe.

Without getting lost in either the images of the poet, or the mathematics of the physicist, it is safe to say all life inherently has rhythm. And, the rhythm of life is inherently found in its deepest resonance – the Song of God. However, to move out of the poetic and hypothetical, the Gospel of John simply and clearly defines Jesus as the Word of God. (John 1). No more difficult to understand theoretical mumbo-jumbo about zero mass and graviton this or that.

The Word of God is made real, human and personal. Jesus is God's Song moving into the neighborhood. By simply arriving in uterus, he's already inspired singing. (Luke 1.46*f*) As he walked through crowds and stood alone, as he reached out and reached down, he was singing God's song. Just as you can share your playlists on Facebook, so Jesus showed up singing God's Song and singing it for you.

Be careful. It's one of those songs that you can't get out of your head. Watch out. It's one of the melodies that put a sway in your hips. Just like learning the alphabet song as a child, the simple tune contains the code for a lifetime of infinite combinations to engage the rhythms of renewal. So it is with the simple song Jesus sings. Forgiveness and freedom form the basic code for all of life's relationships and purpose. From the forgiveness won for us, and the freedom gifted to us, flows a lifetime of infinite combinations to form a lifetime of relationships.

So it is with *The Love Paradox* in Jesus' call to love the Lord your God with all you've got – and love your neighbor as yourself. Beginning with God's love for you, illustrated in the freedom of Jesus, it provides a new self to highly value based on the price Jesus paid to secure your place in eternity. You have complete assurance you are loved. This, in turn provides loving relationship and ministry to your neighbor who then is blessed with God's love through you. Notice the movement and rhythm that repeats across time.

So it is with the caring and tending of your self. It begins with God, who loved you before time. (Romans 8.28*f*) This, in turn equips you with the presence to engage, and the trust to surrender to God all things so you can disengage, become refreshed, and begin again. This rhythm of engaging, disengaging and repeating resembles musical meters grouped in three. Perhaps it feels a little like a waltz. It's as though you're dancing to the beat of eternal music.

The last section of this book continues on the web and is the next invitation for you to first manage yourself well. The web site, "KarlGalik.com" contains recommended links, calendaring and exercises that are helpful – but only to a point. As previously noted, you can read how best and most efficiently to engage life, but if you're not participating in the original rhythm, your energy will deplete, your enthusiasm will wane. All the fruits and vegetables in all the right quantities can certainly do you a world of good, but the best diet cannot transform your soul.

First God transforms your soul – then you share in caring for your soul now transformed by fully engaging, surrendering when you disengage and then doing it over again. First you drink from the Living Waters (John 4.14) then you work hard, play hard and look forward to doing it one more time. First you receive, then you give, then you repeat it in various intensities, with people, places and projects. First you receive God's love shown to you through Jesus, and then you love your neighbor with that same love. First you are loved, and then you love. This is *The Love Paradox*. You receive what God provides because you must first manage yourself well in order to love and lead others.

What does this mean?

The strengthening of the connection between your wellbeing and managing yourself well is realized in this simple elegant rhythm. *Engage. Disengage. Repeat.* Releasing the drive to do too much, the addictive pursuit of more information, and accepting Jesus' gift redeems you for his rhythm – engage, disengage, repeat.

What can you do?

Enjoy the dance. Celebrate the rhythm. Allow yourself to be excited by God's voice calling your name. Accept the love God has for you in Jesus. First, manage yourself well in order to love and lead others. Rest. Then do it again! This is the essence of a joy-filled life!

How to First Manage Yourself Well: Online Resources and Support

KarlGalik.com **Resources**

The Love Paradox Discussion Guide *(free)*

The Love Paradox Blog & Online Community *(free)*

Newsletter *(free)*

The Love Paradox Online Workbook

The Love Paradox Online Small Group Bible Study

Personal Exercises

The Love Paradox Online Guide to Personal Development & Spiritual Growth *(subscription)*

Multi-media Resources

Available Workshops and Speaking Engagements

Links

Notes

ᘓ᠖ᘔ

1. April 2011 <Starbucks.com>

2. Dustin Patterson, January 7, 2010 < http://www.tulsabeacon.com/?p=3432>

3. *The Devil's Advocate,* dir. Taylor Hackford, Full-length feature film, Warner Brothers Production for New Regency Films, 1997.

4. "The Hygiene Hypothesis." November 2010. <www.hygiene-gypothesis.com>

5. Ed Friedman, *Failure of Nerve: Leadership in an Age of Quick Fix.* (Bethesda: The Edwin Friedman Estate/Trust, Bethesda, Maryland. 1999)

6. James Belasco and Ralph Stayer, *"Flight of the Buffalo"* (New York: Warner Books), 312

7. Newton's Third Law of Motion <www.grc.nasa.gov>

8. Alan Klass, *Quiet Conversations: Concrete Help for Weary Ministry Leaders* (Kansas City: Mission Growth Publishing, 2000) 3

9. Peggy Noonan, Wall Street Journal: *Information Overload is Nothing New.* August 20, 2010, <www.onlinewsj.com>

10. William Powers, *Hamlet's Blackberry* (New York: HarperCollins, 2010) 201

11. Basics of Superstring Theory, April 2011 <superstringtheory. com>

CPSIA information can be obtained at www.ICGtesting.com
Printed in the USA
LVOW122036181011

251073LV00002B/4/P